OTHER VOLUMES IN THIS SERIES

THE

BEST

AMERICAN

POETRY

2010

◇   ◇   ◇

Amy Gerstler, Editor

David Lehman, Series Editor

SCRIBNER POETRY

NEW YORK   LONDON   TORONTO   SYDNEY

SCRIBNER POETRY
A Division of Simon & Schuster, Inc.
1230 Avenue of the Americas
New York, NY 10020

First Scribner edition September 2010

For information about special discounts for bulk purchases,
please contact Simon & Schuster Special Sales at 1-866-506-1949
or business@simonandschuster.com.

The Simon & Schuster Speakers Bureau can bring authors to your live event.
For more information or to book an event contact the Simon & Schuster Speakers
Bureau at 1-866-248-3049 or visit our website at www.simonspeakers.com.

Manufactured in the United States of America

1   3   5   7   9   10   8   6   4   2

Library of Congress Control Number: 88644281

ISBN 978-1-4391-8147-8
ISBN 978-1-4391-8145-4 (pbk)
ISBN 978-1-4391-8148-5 (ebook)

CONTENTS

David Lehman was born in New York City in 1948. He was educated at Columbia University and spent two years in England as a Kellett Fellow at Cambridge University. After returning to the United States, he worked as Lionel Trilling's research assistant and received his PhD in English at Columbia in 1978. His books of poetry include *Yeshiva Boys* (2009), *When a Woman Loves a Man* (2005), *The Evening Sun* (2002), *The Daily Mirror* (2000), and *Valentine Place* (1996), all from Scribner. Lehman has edited *The Oxford Book of American Poetry* (Oxford University Press, 2006), *The Best American Erotic Poems: From 1800 to the Present* (Scribner, 2008), and *Great American Prose Poems: From Poe to the Present* (Scribner, 2003). He has written six nonfiction books, most recently *A Fine Romance: Jewish Songwriters, American Songs* (Nextbook/Schocken). He teaches in the graduate writing program of The New School in New York City. He initiated the *Best American Poetry* series in 1988.

FOREWORD

by David Lehman

◇　◇　◇

Over the years I've read novels centering on lawyers, doctors, diplo-mats, teachers, financiers, even car salesmen and dentists, but not until 2009 did I come across one about the travails of the editor of a poetry anthology. When word of *The Anthologist,* Nicholson Baker's new novel, reached me last September, I couldn't wait to read it. Baker's novels defy convention and reveal an obsessive nature, and I wondered what he would make of American poetry, for surely his novel would reflect a strenuous engagement with the art. The title character here, Paul Chowder by unfortunate name, has put together an anthology of poems he is calling *Only Rhyme.* The phrase describes the notional book's contents and indicates the editor's conception of poetic virtue. Paul has chosen the contents of his anthology but is now, on the eve of a deadline, afflicted with writer's block. He needs to write a foreword but cannot. "How many people read introductions to poetry antholo-gies, anyway?" he wonders, then volunteers, "I do, but I'm not normal."

Having asked myself that same question and given a similar answer, I can appreciate the speaker's troubling awareness of the many poets who have to be left out of his book—and the relatively few people who will bother to read his introductory essay. The task of writing a prefatory note becomes no less difficult when it is an annual requirement, though Nicholson Baker may have made my job a little easier this time around. Every editor has the impulse to use the introductory space to open the door, welcome the guest, and disappear without further ado. But some things are worth saying, and one such is Baker's defense of anthologies. For a poet facing all the perils that lurk in a poet's path—a poet very like the novel's Paul Chowder—anthologies represent the possibility of a belated second chance. And it is that possibility, however slim, that spurs the poet to stick to a vocation that offers so much resistance and promises so few rewards. The "you" in these sentences refers to the American poet—and perhaps to American poetry itself, an oddity in an age that worships celebrity. "You think: One more poem. You think: There will be some as yet ungathered anthology of American poetry. It will be the anthology that people tote around with them on subways thirty-five, forty years from now." The poet's conception of fame exists within modest limits, but it is persistent: "And you think: Maybe the very poem I write today will somehow pry open a space in that future anthology and maybe it will drop into position and root itself there."

Baker's skeptical distance from the fray makes his take on things particularly compelling. The opinions he puts forth are provocative and entertaining. A proponent of the sit-com as the great American art form, Baker's anthologist believes that "any random episode of *Friends* is probably better, more uplifting for the human spirit, than ninety-nine percent of the poetry or drama or fiction or history ever published." That is quite a statement, even allowing for the complexity of irony. (After all, to be "uplifting for the human spirit" may not be the ideal criterion by which to judge poetry or history.) The speaker establishes his credentials as an American poet with his realism for self-pity's sake. He suspects that poets form a "community" only in the realm of piety: "We all love the busy ferment, and we all know it's nonsense. Getting together for conferences of international poetry. Hah! A joke. Reading our poems. Our little moment. Physical presence. In the same room with. A community. Forget it. It's a joke."

Baker (or his mouthpiece) likes Swinburne, Poe, Millay, Elizabeth Bishop, Louise Bogan, and the contemporary British poets Wendy Cope and James Fenton. He disapproves of free verse, distrusts the "ultra-extreme enjambment" that you find in William Carlos Williams or Charles Olson, and argues that "iambic pentameter" is something of a hoax. As for the unrhymed poems that dominate literary magazines and university workshops, he feels it would be more accurate to call them "plums" and their authors "plummets" or "plummers." How did we get to this state of affairs? In Baker's account, the chief villain is Ezra Pound, "a blustering bigot—a humorless jokester—a talentless pasticheur—a confidence man." Pound advocated modernism in verse with the same bullying arrogance that went into his radio broadcasts on behalf of Mussolini, and that is no accident, because the impulse that led to fascism also gave rise to modern poetry. Modernism as Pound preached it and T. S. Eliot practiced it—in *The Waste Land,* "a hodge-podge of flummery and borrowed paste"—was, in short, probably as ruinous for the art of verse as fascism was for Europe. The popularity of translations, especially prose versions of exotic foreign verse rendered from a language that the translator doesn't know, also did its part to hasten the "death of rhyme."

The views articulated in *The Anthologist* are antithetical to contemporary practice in ways that recall Philip Larkin's conviction that Pound ruined poetry, Picasso ruined painting, and Charlie Parker ruined jazz: the dissenting position, pushed to an amusing extreme, and stated with uncompromising intelligence. The narrator can sound a sour note. To teach creative writing to college students is to be "a professional teller of lies," he maintains, gleefully quoting Elizabeth Bishop on the subject: "I think one of the worst things I know about modern education is this 'Creative Writing' business." Nevertheless Baker's opinions are worth pondering, especially when the "difficulty versus accessibility" question becomes the subject of debate. And his advice to the aspiring poet is astute. Don't postpone writing the poem, he says. "Put it down, work on it, finish it. If you don't get on it now, somebody else will do something similar, and when you crack open next year's *Best American Poetry* and see it under somebody else's name you'll hate yourself."

The Anthologist was well received and prominently reviewed in book supplements that rarely notice poetry books, let alone anthologies of them, except with a certain contempt, which was a mild irony but an old story. Some laudatory articles went so far as to declare that "you" will enjoy the work "even if you generally couldn't care less about verse." But then, when poetry or the teaching of poetry is discussed, commentators have a hard time avoiding a note of condescension. Poetry is called a "lost art." It is thought to be something young people go through, a phase; something you have to apologize for, as when a poet at a reading reassures the audience that only three more poems remain on the docket. And yet poetry retains its prestige. The term exists as a sort of benchmark in fields ranging from politics to athletics. Columnists enjoy reminding newly elected officials that "you campaign in poetry but govern in prose"—an axiom that aligns poetry on the side of idealism and eloquence against the bureaucratic details and inconveniences of prosaic administration. In the *Financial Times,* the Czech photographer Miroslav Tichý, who spied on women with his homemade viewfinder, "stealing their likenesses as they giggled, gossiped and dreamed," is described as "a peeping Tom with a poet's eye." Of Nancy Pelosi, readers of *Time* learned that, to the Speaker's credit, when a colleague's mother dies, she "encloses a poem written by her own mother with her condolence." In the same issue of the magazine, a flattering profile of General Stanley McChrystal, commander of U.S.

forces in Afghanistan, appeared. During the Iraq war, McChrystal sent copies of "The Second Coming" to his special operators, challenging them to flip the meaning of Yeats's lines: "The best lack all conviction, while the worst / Are full of passionate intensity."

Has there ever been a really good movie about a poet as opposed to the many excellent movies in which poetry is quoted to smart effect? *Bright Star*, Jane Campion's film about the ill-starred romance of John Keats and the barely legal Fanny Brawne, came out in 2009 and showed there is life left in the familiar stereotype of the consumptive poet burning a fever for love. Campion won over Quentin Tarantino. "The movie made me think about taking a writing class," the director of *Pulp Fiction* said. "One of the best things that can happen from a movie about an author is that you actually want to read their work." On television, poetry continues to put in regular appearances on *The PBS NewsHour* with Jim Lehrer and sometimes sneaks into scripted shows. When an advertising copywriter on *Mad Men* loses his job, he doesn't take it well. He "did not go gentle into that good night," an ex-associate observes. The critic Stephen Burt believes that *Project Runway* holds some useful lessons for poetry critics: "*Project Runway* even recalls the famous exercises in 'practical criticism' performed at the University of Cambridge in the 1920s, in which professor I. A. Richards asked his students to make snap judgments about unfamiliar poems." I have commented on the inspired way that quotations from poems turn up in classic Hollywood movies, and if you're lucky enough to catch *It's Always Fair Weather* the next time Robert Osborne shows it on TCM, you'll see a superb 1950s movie musical (music by André Previn, book and lyrics by Betty Comden and Adolph Green) that sums itself up brilliantly in three lines from *As You Like It* that enliven a conversation between Gene Kelly and Cyd Charisse:

> Most friendship is feigning, most loving mere folly.
> Then heigh-ho, the holly!
> This life is most jolly.

Meanwhile, you can't pull the wool over the creative writers responsible for *Law and Order: Criminal Intent*. In a 2009 episode, a celebrated campus bard is murdered by his ex-girlfriend, who is handy with a knife. Has he been pimping out his attractive young assistants to wealthy donors? After learning how rotten the poets are to one another, the major case squad detective says that if her daughter ever says she wants to be a poet, she'd tell her to join the Mafia instead: "Nicer people." As convalescents confined to hospital beds know, you can go wall to wall with reruns of *Law and Order,* and sure enough, the day after this episode aired I saw a rerun of *Law and Order: Criminal Intent,* in which the villain is a nerdy insurance man, an actuary with Asperger's syndrome, whose name is Wallace Stevens. The detectives call him Wally affectionately. I spent the rest of my bedridden day with Stevens's collected poems.

Haaretz, Israel's oldest Hebrew-language daily, turned over its pages entirely to poets and novelists for one day in June 2009. The results were unsurprising in some ways (a lot of first-person point of view) but inventive and unconventional in the coverage of the stock market ("everything okay") and the weather (a sonnet likening summer to an unsharpened pencil). The experiment reminded me of W. S. Di Piero's assertion that the writing of good prose is the acid test of a poet's intelligence. "Some shy from putting prose out there because it's a giveaway," Di Piero has written. "You can't fake it. It reveals quality of mind, for better or worse, in a culture where poems can be faked. Find a faker and ask him or her to write anything more substantial than a jacket blurb, and the jig is up." When we posted Di Piero's remark on the *Best American Poetry* blog, Sally Ashton added an apt simile (a poem can be faked "like an orgasm") and a few inevitable questions ("Who is fooled? Who benefits?"). Speaking of the *BAP* blog, there are days when it resembles nothing so much as a cross-cultural newspaper written by poets and poetry lovers. Recent visitors to the *BAP* blog could read Catharine Stimpson's reaction to homicidal violence at the University of Alabama; Lewis Saul's meticulously annotated commentary on thirty films by Akira Kurosawa; Jennifer Michael Hecht's heartfelt plea to poets contemplating the suicide of Rachel Wetzsteon ("don't kill yourself"); Laura Orem's obituaries for Lucille Clifton, Jean Simmons, and J. D. Salinger; Katha Pollitt on Berlin in the fall; Larry Epstein on Bob Dylan; Ken Tucker on new books of poetry; Todd Swift on young British poets; Phoebe Putnam on the covers poets choose for their books; Mitch Sisskind's "poetic tips of the day" (e.g., "Secrecy sustains the world"); Gabrielle Calvocoressi at the sports desk; Terence Winch on Irish American music; Stacey Harwood on *nocino,* the Italian liqueur made from under-ripe green walnuts; and a James Cummins epigram entitled "Anti-Confessional": "What it was like, I don't recall, or care to; / believe me, you should be grateful I spare you."

The Best American Poetry anthology itself, now in its twenty-third year, remains committed to the idea that American poetry is as vital as it is various and that it is possible to capture the spirit of its diversity and a measure of its excellence in an annual survey of our magazines, in print or online. As the selections are made by a different editor each year, each a distinguished practitioner, the series has inevitably become an annotated chronicle of the taste of our leading poets. I persuaded Amy Gerstler to make the selections for the 2010 edition of *The Best American Poetry* because of my delight in her poems and my respect for her judgment, and it was wonderful to work with her. Amy's new book, *Dearest Creature,* came out last year, and augmented her reputation as arguably the most inventive and ambitious poet of her generation. Gerstler can be very funny without forfeiting her right to be taken seriously; she has a quality of sincerity, of truth-telling, that can coexist with the most sophisticated of comic sensibilities. Her poems of deep feeling may take on an insouciant disguise: a letter to a cherished niece about the virtues of an encyclopedia, a conversation between a black taffeta and strapless pink dress, a riff consisting entirely of slang phrases from the not too distant past. Yet always at the heart of the poetry is an insight into the human condition and the ability to state it simply and powerfully: "Some of us grow up doing / credible impressions of model citizens / (though sooner or later hairline / cracks appear in our facades). The rest / get dubbed eccentrics, unnerved and undone / by other people's company, for which we / nevertheless pine." David Kirby reviewed *Dearest Creature* in *The New York Times Book Review*. "Gerstler is skilled in every kind of comedy, from slapstick to whimsy," Kirby wrote. "Yet there's a deep seriousness in every one of these poems, like the plaintive 'Midlife Lullaby,' in which the cow who is now the meatloaf in somebody's sandwich speaks of life's passing pleasures as hauntingly as one of those skeletons who tend to pop up in medieval allegories to remind young knights of their mortality." Kirby concluded his review with a ringing endorsement: "In Amy Gerstler I trust."

The world has been slow to react to the case of Saw Wai, the imprisoned Burmese poet who was arrested two years ago for publishing a love poem for Valentine's Day with a secret message critical of Burma's military dictator, Than Shwe. But the story refuses to die, and the anonymously translated poem itself has now been published (in *Pen America*) and reprinted (in *Harper's,* in February 2010). What early journalistic accounts called a "straightforward" or "innocuous" love poem turns out to be something much richer and stranger. Entitled "February 14," Saw Wai's poem, which appeared in the Rangoon magazine *The Love*

Journal, was initially said to have been a torch song to the fashion model who rejected the poet but taught him the meaning of love. Nothing of the sort. It exemplifies rather a particular strain of modernist poetry, the leading-edge poems of the 1930s that were aped (and perfected) by the Australian hoax poet Ern Malley. The poem is an acrostic—that is, the first letters of the lines, when read down vertically, spell out a message, and in this case that message is, "General Than Shwe is power crazy." In Burmese, Than means "million" and Shwe means "gold," so when Saw Wai concludes his poem with the injunction "Millions of people / Who know how to love / Please clap your gilded hands / And laugh out loud," he is secretly urging his compatriots to laugh the "power crazy" head of the junta off the stage. It took courage to write these lines. It also took an extraordinary talent for modern poetry considered as a kind of cipher, and the result in its English translation might be read as either a brief for the methods of modernism or a textbook illustration of what Nicholson Baker would have us see as the tempting dangers of the non-rhyming, prose-saturated "plum":

> Arensberg said:[1]
> Only once you have experienced deep pain
> And madness
> And like an adolescent
> Thought the blurred photo of a model
> Great art
> Can you call it heartbreak.
> Millions of people
> Who know how to love
> Please clap your gilded hands
> And laugh out loud.

1. Walter Conrad Arensberg, the noted art collector and donor of great paintings to the Philadelphia Museum of Art, wrote *The Cryptography of Shakespeare* (1922), purporting to find, in the Bard's plays, anagrams and acrostics that prove Francis Bacon's authorship. Arensberg wrote symbolist-influenced poetry, but it is conceivable that spurious cryptography is his real contribution to the radical element in modern poetry.

Amy Gerstler was born in San Diego, California, in 1956. A writer of poetry, nonfiction, and journalism, she won the National Book Critics Circle Award in poetry for *Bitter Angel* in 1991. Penguin published her most recent book of poems, *Dearest Creature,* in 2009. Her previous twelve books include *Ghost Girl, Medicine, Crown of Weeds,* which won a California Book Award, and *Nerve Storm.* Gerstler received a Durfee Foundation Artists Award in 2002. She has contributed reviews and articles to *Artforum, The Village Voice, Los Angeles* magazine, the *Los Angeles Times, Bookforum,* and *Art and Antiques.* She is a member of the core faculty of the Bennington Writing Seminars MFA program at Bennington College in Vermont. She also teaches in the graduate fine arts department at Art Center College of Design, in Pasadena, California, and in the master of professional writing program at the University of Southern California. She lives in Los Angeles.

INTRODUCTION

by Amy Gerstler

FEED YOUR HEAD

Ever since my father died of a heart attack, in April 2002, I have accompanied my mother to the opera, taking Dad's place next to her in the balcony's topmost velvet seats, also known as the nosebleed section. My mother, now eighty, studied voice as a girl and contemplated a career in musical theater. Opera is among her sustaining joys. It is one of her lifelong loves, a balm and a passion that, despite widowhood, crippling arthritis, and other age-related tribulations, makes her want to stay alive.

When my mother (whose name is Mimi, like the consumptive waif in *La Bohème*) listens to a particularly beautiful aria, live or recorded, often she will weep. To see Mimi at such moments is to witness a fellow being in the throes of transcendence. I hope that the poems in this anthology might provide readers with a similar thrill, an experience analogous to what my mother feels when she listens to Russian soprano Anna Netrebko. The poems assembled here had something like that effect on me, which is why I picked them. And on multiple readings they continue to cause my synapses to quicken and to give me that "going up!" elevator sensation.

If opera is too esoteric a comparison for you, or if you side with my friend C., an otherwise intelligent woman who can't understand why anyone would willingly spend a night at the opera, "listening to all that yowling," I'll put it another way. I'll liken these poems to versions of the sensual, cerebral rapture that food critic Jonathan Gold describes when he's confronted with "the strong, dark meat of wild boar, with its divine stink of the woods in fall" or "the delicate smoky sweetness of roasted figs . . . set like a jewel on a bit of grilled bread." It's no accident that Gold turns to poetry when reporting on his revelations at table. Poetry is uniquely empowered to praise. Poetry can describe, engage and/or detonate delight via mind and ear. It can contain immensities and paradoxes we experience at peak moments. There are times when nothing less than poetry will do. In lauding a cocktail made from gin, fresh lemon, and a squirt of violet essence, Gold invokes lines from D. H. Lawrence's poem "Craving for Spring." "If you catch a whiff of violets from the darkness of the shadow of man, / it will be spring in the world."

I teach a class for college students that often amounts to "Poetry for Non-Poets." I enjoy doing this because, like many of my colleagues, I consider myself a cheerleader for the genre, and am zealous (and pretty shameless) about winning converts for my church. One of the first statements I make when class meets is that I believe saying you don't care for poetry is like saying you don't care for food. An annoyingly picky eater, I can't stand the smell of liver, and detest all melons (they taste like watered-down perfume to me). Fortunately, there are so many other delicacies in the world! And luckily for us, poems of high quality continue to be written, in every form and, I'm tempted to say, flavor. A little investigation, fueled by courage, curiosity, and appetite, will turn up poetry that will "feed your head," to quote Jefferson Airplane's song "White Rabbit," no matter what sort of head you have. Plenty of poems housed in this anthology could (and perhaps should) be described in palate-whetting terms like those used to characterize wines: *this poem's jazzy aromas and flavors of blueberry and plum, with subtle black pepper back notes, contribute color, complexity, and depth to the overall composition.* I half wish the setup of this book had permitted me to insert descriptive menu entries for each poem, to steer readers toward what might best suit their literary taste buds.

So—I hope this volume will arouse (and maybe satisfy) hungers, be gnawed on for a good long time, and have effects not unlike those of your favorite handmade vodka or exquisite dish of risi e bisi. I also have a more pointed, ambitious hope up my sleeve, which I have more than hinted at. I badly want this anthology to be read not only by poetry fans, but also by famished souls who never dreamed they'd admire any text that called itself a poem. I'm not sure how to accomplish this. The publisher has not empowered me to give away thousands of free copies, dropping them from prop planes and blimps. The press run for this book is not going to be large enough to accommodate such a propaganda blitz, anyway. Nevertheless, I would love for this anthology to function as a gateway drug for the poetically resistant, uninitiated, or just plain scared. I'd like it to provide heady textual adventures that both the confirmed poetry parishioner and the new convert can savor.

Recently, when asked how she liked a magnificently sung opera we had just seen, my mother responded, "I was so proud of the human race!" The poems in this book make me feel the same way. And now that I've come clean about my missionary intentions, I'll move on.

You may be faintly curious what it's like to edit one of these suckers. Honestly, folks, the hardest part was not making this a twenty-six-volume set. It could have been an encyclopedia. I read zillions of amazing poems. They were spread all over the floor, and the cat sat on them, sifting his fine black fur onto stanza after stanza, sometimes shredding edges of single sheets with his claws when I withdrew them from under his rump too quickly. There were days when, terrified by the mounting piles of journals and reviews the postman delivered daily, I dreaded entering my small office. Eventually, as the process neared its end, I was walled in by stacks of literary magazines, like some hapless sinner in an Edgar Allan Poe story. And in the midst of this overdose, this glut, this engulfing avalanche, this embarrassment of riches, I fell in love with poetry all over again.

America is awash in fabulous literary magazines, of every shape, size, and aesthetic stripe. Many have charming or amusing names, artsy covers, or origami-like folds. Editing any literary magazine, much less a good one, requires an incredible amount of work, and writers who devote their time to this endeavor deserve a special tier in heaven. Despite the mild, shuddering case of publication phobia I developed toward the end of the judging period, breaking into a sweat whenever I glimpsed so much as a copy of *TV Guide,* I now find myself in a kind of mourning that my yearlong free subscriptions to these heaps of stellar magazines are kaput. (In the past few weeks, they have all sent me renewal notices. Believe me, worthy journals, I'd subscribe to you all if I could!) Likewise, scores of poems that I could not include still cause me spasms of regret. My solace is that I can teach and reread and recommend and tack to my office wall and e-mail these poems to my heart's content. And while I am bemoaning the not-included, I will issue a public apology to my teaching colleagues. To avoid conflict of interest, I decided not to include poems by anyone I currently teach with at the three colleges where I'm employed.

Seventy-five poems, the magic limit for this anthology, is a very small number, especially given the happy fact that, in my view, American poetry is in the exact opposite condition of the tattered American economy. Just to say it: American poetry, based on my temperature-taking researches all last year, is rich, vital, beguiling, and smart; packed with talented, inventive, all-over-the-map practitioners and great diversity of forms, methods, subjects, and voices. No stolen valor here. Rather, much valor of many hues, and all of it earned.

A word about taste. When I began this yearlong process of, to quote the late great David Foster Wallace, "deciderization," I was determined to do my best to represent the entire range of American poetry at the present time. There would be poems of every school, persuasion, and methodology included! I would read from sea to shining sea to find them! Looking back through the anthology as it stands now, I am once again whacked in the head by what I realized not very far into the process: that I could no more escape my own proclivities, preferences, and tastes when editing this book than I can when writing my own poems.

In a way, working on the anthology turned out to be more akin to writing a poem than I would ever have guessed. Themes, modes, and ideas I've long been obsessed with: women's bodies and lives, sex, dogs, the devil, the dead, lists, drugs (psychotropic and otherwise), disease, epistolary literature, prayers, coming of age, dregs, graveyards, ghosts, religion, insanity, love, animals, drunkenness, mordant wit, and other pet topics long resident in the pest house of my head make multiple appearances here. Sometimes during the process of assembling the anthology when I got very lost and overwhelmed, as I often do when writing, it felt almost as though the book began to exert a burgeoning will of its own, with its own hungers, tidal pulls, quirks, and requirements, just as it sometimes feels when a poem I am wrestling with is taking shape. As the deadline approached, I changed the final lineup over a dozen times, just as I find myself repeatedly removing and reinserting lines when writing a poem. Even which poem would open the book and which would end it (to an extent predetermined because this is an alphabetical anthology) was something I fussed over as I do the first and last lines of poems I'm writing.

Prose poems have always intrigued me. I feel they are a fertile direction in American poetry and they are amply represented here. If someone wants to revive that weary old argument about how prose poems are not legitimate poetry, buy me a drink and I'll politely listen to your views. But my hunch is that my predilection for poems that are transgendered, oops, I meant trans-genred, will survive the encounter. They continue to fascinate me, and make me dizzy with possibilities.

Back to taste. I'm not saying this would be the case with every editor in this situation, but for me, once I stopped trying to fight my own leanings and succumbed to the idea that my taste was my sharpest tool, and that if I was going to edit this thing, I was going to have to make maximum use of it, the job got a little easier and a lot more doable. The wishful delusion I am so often prey to, that some new move or activity (getting a radical haircut, learning German, doing an enemy a favor, becoming Buddhist, editing an anthology) is going to transform me, and allow me to operate as a different being in the wide world, died the same quick, violent death it always does right out of the gate. I was going to have to edit the anthology as me, and do the best job I could under the circumstances.

Except it wasn't quite so bad, because I got to work with series editor David Lehman, who has the energy and enthusiasm of a championship baseball team, as well as mad editing skills, and to whom I owe bottomless thanks. And I was occasionally consoled by this remark Allen Ginsberg made about his own poems: "My intention was to make a picture of the mind, mistakes and all." I liked the idea that a poem and maybe an anthology, too, could work as some kind of functional MRI. An anthology is a picture of many things, but it cannot fail to be a snapshot of the anthologist's mind.

An anthology can also provide a shadowy likeness of its time. Zeitgeist-y concerns and images that crop up in this sample of American poems of 2009 include: race, the "wars" in Iraq and Afghanistan, the use of lithium and Zoloft, AIDS, "presidential blackness," sex education, religious fundamentalism, divorce, condoms, new views of motherhood, prison, depression, end times, fidelity, standardized tests. Several poems feature breasts. And the careless and selfish way we have polluted and nearly destroyed the earth has not escaped the notice of our poets.

This anthology is likely also a picture of my needs as a reader, which I like to believe are shared by many of my fellows. "When peoples care for you and cry for you, they can straighten out your soul." So wrote Langston Hughes. Reading these poems helped straighten out my soul, which is in constant need of such ministrations. Reading these poems also jogged me to remember that I want to act as though I have a soul, despite the fact that it sometimes goes missing. Toward the end of the D. H. Lawrence poem quoted above, he uses the phrase "wonderment organizing itself," which seems another apt description of what poetry does, and what it provides that we need. Lose touch with wonderment and you're fucked. You start to wizen like a prune, and pretty soon you're dried up and lifeless. Sights, sounds, thoughts, and perceptions flood by in a barely noticed, monochromatic blur. You have misplaced the capacity to be amazed.

Humor is another touchstone I never want to lose sight of as writer or reader. This being so, it's no surprise that the comic exerted a strong pull on me as editor. Of course I don't believe all poems must contain comic elements to succeed, but I am often drawn to those that do, and consider comedy a saving grace. I think humor in poetry can be a form of courage, when poets are willing to rock poetry's temple walls with serious, meaningful, ringing laughter—that odd sound so similar in its gasping heaves to sobs. In his treatise on jokes Freud remarked, "It may happen . . . that the best achievements in the way of jokes are used as an envelope for thoughts of the greatest substance." And in an essay entitled "Some Remarks on Humor" E. B. White wrote, "If a humorous piece of writing brings a person to the point where his emotional responses are untrustworthy and seem likely to break over into the opposite realm, it is because humor, like poetry, has an extra content. It plays close to the big hot fire which is Truth, and sometimes the reader feels the heat." Right on, E.B.! So when those two sources of heat and light, poetry and comedy, manage to join forces, searing illuminations may take place. I think many of the poems in this anthology use humor in this way: to question, to pull reality apart in ways that jolt us into perceptual shifts, propelling us to reassemble ourselves and our dearly held assumptions. Caricature, satire, mockery, absurdity, wit, and irony can be social, emotional, and political disinfectants. They represent some of protest's most deadly weapons, and are powerful antidotes to complacency or indifference. Baudelaire, in his essay on laughter, refers to the humorless as "spiteful pundits of solemnity" and "charlatans of gravity." Surely we do not want poems or poets to fall prey to such accusations.

Poetry also serves other darker, maybe more complicated needs, which I have neither space nor inclination to explore here. I will just say that in ancient Mesopotamia, a culture perhaps not so different from our own, there were five basic job descriptions for poets:

1. astrologer/scribe
2. diviner
3. exorcist/magician
4. physician
5. lamentation chanter

This last, "lamentation chanter," is probably the post I would choose. And which one best suits you, dear reader? We read and compose poems to soothe our babies, to chat up the gods, to remember what happened yesterday and back in 2,500 BCE, and to muse about what changes and what never will. We use poems to accuse and beguile the dead, to dismantle language like a kid taking apart a radio to see where the voices and static come from: fiddling with transistors and tinkering with linguistic impulses. We leave posterity, that most speculative of audiences, notes in the forms of poems. Our tribe of upright monkeys will always require specially charged, compressed language bursts that marry prayer and play, so we will never be without blessings, spells, curses, cures, protests, tongue twisters, riddles, hymns, vows, recipes, threats, boasts, apologies, pleas, insults, predictions, taunts, rants, or dirges. We climb several stories in the dead of night to scribble poems onto billboards that are later deemed graffiti. We e-mail, tweet, and text them to friends. Even schoolchildren know: ever since we invented language or it invented us, we chiseled poems into stone, sang them, pressed texts into wet clay tablets, then invented paper to transcribe and transport them. We rap and digitize poetic texts every day. We chant them in mosques or at gravesides or during weeklong retreats. We exhale them in puffs of smoke during pipe ceremonies or when we say kaddish or while panting after sex as heart rates slow and mingled fluids dry. We have been known to sneak poems out of prisons and death camps at the risk of our lives. Presidents, popes, and ayatollahs quote them. But you know all this. As Gertrude Stein wrote in her essay "Poetry and Grammar," "Poetry will also always always be with us . . . Poetry like prose has lived through a good deal."

My original idea for this introduction (which I scrapped, because I do not want to be labeled a slacker) was that it should consist in its entirety of this one sentence from Keats's letters:

"Here are the Poems—they will explain themselves—as all poems should do without any comment."

Later, after I'd composed some paragraphs, I thought I would end the essay with that quote. That was until moments ago, when this morsel of spam, a poem in sheep's clothing, arrived via e-mail, from India. I have broken the sentences into line lengths.

> This company mainly sells
> the motor, the computer,
> the television, the handset
> and so on, & its quality may obtain

the guarantee. If you have need
please to enter the website.
Anticipates your presence!

   The text calls to mind two languages, hastily mating. As fiction writer Donald Barthelme wrote, "Bless Babel."
   This anthology anticipates your presence! Welcome.

THE
BEST
AMERICAN
POETRY
2010

◇   ◇   ◇

DICK ALLEN

What You Have to Get Over

◊   ◊   ◊

Stumps. Railroad tracks. Early sicknesses,
the blue one, especially.
Your first love rounding a corner,
that snowy minefield.

Whether you step lightly or heavily,
you have to get over to that tree line a hundred yards in the distance
before evening falls,
letting no one see you wend your way,

that wonderful, old-fashioned word, *wend,*
meaning "to proceed, to journey,
to travel from one place to another,"
as from bed to breakfast, breakfast to imbecile work.

You have to get over your resentments,
the sun in the morning and the moon at night,
all those shadows of yourself you left behind
on odd little tables.

Tote that barge! Lift that bale! You have to
cross that river, jump that hedge, surmount that slogan,
crawl over this ego or that eros,
then hoist yourself up onto that yonder mountain.

Another old-fashioned word, *yonder,* meaning
"that indicated place, somewhere generally seen
or just beyond sight." If you would recover,
you have to get over the shattered autos in the backwoods lot

1

to that bridge in the darkness
where the sentinels stand
guarding the border with their half-slung rifles,
warned of the likes of you.

from *The Hudson Review*

JOHN ASHBERY

Alcove

◇　　◇　　◇

Is it possible that spring could be
once more approaching? We forget each time
what a mindless business it is, porous like sleep,
adrift on the horizon, refusing to take sides, "mugwump
of the final hour," lest an agenda—horrors!—be imputed to it,
and the whole point of its being spring collapse
like a hole dug in sand. It's breathy, though,
you have to say that for it.

And should further seasons coagulate
into years, like spilled, dried paint, why,
who's to say we weren't provident? We indeed
looked out for others as though they mattered, and they,
catching the spirit, came home with us, spent the night
in an alcove from which their breathing could be heard clearly.
But it's not over yet. Terrible incidents happen
daily. That's how we get around obstacles.

from *London Review of Books*

Unit of Measure

◇　◇　◇

All can be measured by the standard of the capybara.
Everyone is lesser than or greater than the capybara.
Everything is taller or shorter than the capybara.
Everything is mistaken for a Brazilian dance craze
more or less frequently than the capybara.
Everyone eats greater or fewer watermelons
than the capybara. Everyone eats more or less bark.
Everyone barks more than or less than the capybara,
who also whistles, clicks, grunts, and emits what is known
as his *alarm squeal*. Everyone is more or less alarmed
than a capybara, who—because his back legs
are longer than his front legs—feels like
he is going downhill at all times.
Everyone is more or less a *master of grasses*
than the capybara. Or going by the scientific name,
more or less *Hydrochoerus hydrochaeris*—
or, going by the Greek translation, more or less
water hog. Everyone is more or less
of a fish than the capybara, defined as the outermost realm
of fishdom by the 16th-century Catholic Church.
Everyone is eaten more or less often for Lent than
the capybara. Shredded, spiced, and served over plantains,
everything tastes more or less like pork
than the capybara. Before you decide that you are
greater than or lesser than a capybara, consider
that while the Brazilian capybara breeds only once a year,
the Venezuelan variety mates continuously.
Consider the last time you mated continuously.
Consider the year of your childhood when you had

exactly as many teeth as the capybara—
twenty—and all yours fell out, and all his
kept growing. Consider how his skin stretches
in only one direction. Accept that you are stretchier
than the capybara. Accept that you have foolishly
distributed your eyes, ears, and nostrils
all over your face. Accept that now you will never be able
to sleep underwater. Accept that the fish
will never gather to your capybara body offering
their soft, finned love. *One of us,* they say, *one of us,*
but they will not say it to you.

from *Poetry*

The Devil You Don't

◇   ◇   ◇

He started out as just
a wayward scrap of light

and now consumes
whatever he chooses,
cutting a stolen strain

of lyrical ease with his own.
His heart

rolls into the palm of his hand
and waits there like a blister

in a tree.

▲

The faint alluring radiance

that twitches
over the black seafloor,
held up
by a fish made of teeth

and to which are drawn smaller things—
this is how he tries to love.

Were he to put flesh
on you, it would be flame.

Were he to pick you up
then drop you, all through

the burning sky would you fall.
And burning still you would rip

a hole in the sea, the boiling sea.

⋏

He turns angels
into the same fire that melts
the guts of the earth

or spews unbearably out of stars,
then makes of their wings endless

chains from which to swing.
When the planet's fontanel yields

to his fingerings, he rides, rides,
covers his ears against
a rumor he cannot bear.

His aliases crackle
over the airport speakers,

but they are nowhere
and are never going home.

⋏

Not for a moment
does he wish for
us to give up our gods. *Renounce,*

he says and shrugs, *renounce and still
you die and nothing else.* But no one

is listening—the poor have stopped,
    the rest likely never began.

Here's the best way to see a thing: catch
    the edge of light
        that burns

around its opposite, that
        which it would otherwise
obscure. If we could view

this light entire, we would call it
god—but then, if we saw collected

    in one place
    all the ants or all
    the abandoned cars or all the dust

      in the world, we would surely
      make that thing god instead.

▲

I am going to pull the music
from your mouth and furthermore

I'll take the orange aching light that splits
    your ribs when I or any
beautiful things come at you.

▲

He rolls by on a skateboard, chased by
snakes of smoke. Helicopters rear

and waver all around him, gusting
    down the avenue,
    toward the fissured monuments,
    kicking up a blast
of helices that settle like pollen

                    in a glittering layer
            over everyone. He adores
                the show, the high

    tech of it, the low—but don't broach
                evil, don't bore him so.
                        Clearly this is no Saint

    Paddy's Day parade and he's neither
    headed off to some seminar

                nor giving you the eye.

                        ▲

                He's going to stick
                    to the roof
        of someone's mouth—American

                palate, quintessential mistrust.

    He writes fortunes in clear
                lip gloss on a funhouse mirror

            as the oracles take down their tents
        and their oracular fountains

    bubble in the rimy night. One finger
                    in. *Now say*
                what you want
                        more than anything else.

                        ▲

    From serrated streaks of fire
                he fashions
                a subcutaneous matrix,

    sightlines to further green
            vistas. The tributes

of the origamists don't last long, but the sound

of burning swans

blown down a path to the river
makes music enough for him.

▲

Kids roll hash into
their cigarettes and spotlights
turn the smoke pink
in the trees. If he'd had

a childhood, he'd have spent it

running under sprinklers
to cool his smoldering skin. He made

other arrangements
and found no need for cruelty
in his hell-as-metaphor,

wherein he was more often tempted
than the tempter, watching evolution, each

new thing. Now admirers call
him up to say they'd seen him

on TV and are preparing another

way—such is the devotion
he endures
as everywhere a boiling dew

saturates the buildings till they fall.

▲

Oppenheim's cup and the smell
         of static arouse him—what other
              distortions has he surmounted,
within what circles
    of pleasure has he flexed?
                 The powers that bore
    have flown in from the East,
     a locust wave blotting out
     the scenery. Their bodies pile up
      in black drifts through which
       he later slaloms. Plastic flowers
                warp in the crematorium,
                    smother the undertaker
        with their fumes.

                    ▲

         As he rearranges
              body parts, the sex

grows gigantic, the messiest yet. Take him
                      by the tail and see better

     at night. Swiveling armatures, nothing's
     your misdeed; randy boy and roguish,

          looking for a light,
      watch the wind turn
to whips that tangle in the stars,

           his gift to you.

                    ▲

He strides through a field of rubies
         as comets trail

from his horns. Astronauts
          mistake the streaks

for a runway somewhere safe—this
is the version they invent when

we pull them from the trees
and send them home.

▲

Did the president just say,
"I readjust my horned suit,"
causing our screens to flush
and flicker blood?

On American highways, cars hydroplane
through the acid foam
that slides from blazing
angels' flanks. When the press
corps cranes its collective neck
to get a better view,

the devil turns water in the glass
under the lectern to steam,

then absconds with his toy
piano under one arm
and a seashell pressed
to his glowing mouth, leaving

the president who is not the president
trapped in a red room.

▲

You can pretend I live in a burning box
underground,

that you'd know me if you saw
me, but I don't

and you never do.

His smile is an electric fence
                spitting an amazement
of scarlet flowers into the night.

Hell also has a sky, the world
        being devoured by the sun.

⟶

        Abominable fancy, slide us across
                        the burning lawns.

That which doesn't kill us
        is merely waiting;
                it will.

Flattery will get you started, boy.

Hell is coming. *Hell is here.*

from *The New York Quarterly*

TODD BOSS

My Dog Has No Nose

◊   ◊   ◊

for beauty. She
knows not where it

nests, nor how it
flushes and goes,
nor how best

to close it
in her mouth's
soft wallet, nor

whether, if she
brought it and
laid it at the feet

of her lord, he'd
mete out any but
the usual reward.

from *The Georgia Review*

The Dead

◇   ◇   ◇

The dead are disorderly. If they rot, worms;
if cremated, a waste of smoke. Maybe rot
is better. For where does fire-energy go? I see
energy transferred to worms and so on. But fire
speeds up molecules, then they slow down.
Worms can sometimes turn into winged things.
Good grief, I'm here on the dock thinking how best
to be dead! A dead fish lies on the lake bottom,
white belly up, quickly absorbed into the under-
world. The day's getting warmer. The day depends
upon the release of energy from the dead, whatever
has turned itself over to this rising. Triple layers:
earth, water, air—transversed only by those
who've taken the plunge, so to speak. I'm caught,
my foot in the bear-trap of living. Mother's grave
is sinking, the cheap casket. We've betrayed her
once again. I feel her feeling, the suffering she
feels in there, the dirt, the disorder. She'll never
be smoke; she's heavier, sadder. I don't want to
talk about this. People who talk about abstractions
are like jet-trails that gradually disperse. Others
rot. They are loved by worms. Sad as it is, it's
more exacting. There are bones, fingernails, hair,
and then the bones go, and the hair looks like dirt.
The dirt is happy and the body is happy
to be opened, after a lifetime of nail biting. It loves
the way the air filters through, like carbonation.
It feels that it cannot feel. The not-feeling is like
not-being, only more so: it is being all the way

through, nothing to get in the way. Here come
four ducklings, there used to be five, still downy,
with their mother. I imagine the fifth one, the quick
turtle's jaw, the bloop under, the mother's wild
circling, then all settling, easy. The rest want me
to feed them. They bob in a nice neat row.

from *Southern Poetry Review*

Wildly Constant

◊   ◊   ◊

Sky before dawn is blackish green.
Perhaps a sign.
I should learn more about signs.

Turning a corner to the harbour
the wind hits me
a punch in the face.

I always walk in the morning,
I don't know why anymore.
Life is short.

My shadow goes before me.
With its hood up
it looks like a foghorn.

Ice on the road.
Ice on the sidewalk.
Nowhere to step.

It's better to step
where the little black stones are.
Not so slippery.

I guess the little black stones
could be lava.
Or do I exoticise.

A man hurries past
with a small dog.
No one says Hello.

A pink schoolgirl passes.
Looks in my face.
No one says Hello.

Who would expect
to see a walking foghorn
out so early.

Wind pushes more.
I push back.
Almost home.

Why did I come here.
New wind every day.
Life is for pushing back.

Now it is dawn.
A gold eyelid opens
over the harbour.

People who live here
learn not to complain
about the wind.

I go inside and make tea.
Eat bran flakes.
Read three pages of Proust.

Proust is complaining
(it is 1914)
about the verb *savoir* as used by journalists.

He says they use it
not as a sign of the future
but as a sign of their desires—

sign of what they want the future to be.
What's wrong with that? I think.
I should learn more about signs.

The first thing I saw
the first morning I went out for a walk in Stykkishólmur
was a crow

as big as a chair.
What's that chair doing on top of that house? I thought
then it flapped away.

A crow that big is called a raven.
Corvus corax is Linnaeus's binomial system.
Each one makes a sound

like a whole townful of ravens
in the country I come from.
Three adjectives that recur

in the literature on ravens are
omnivorous.
Pernicious.

Monogamous.
I'm interested in monogamous.
I got married last May

and had my honeymoon in Stykkishólmur.
This year I returned to Stykkishólmur
to live with my husband

for three months in one small room.
This extreme monogamy
proved almost too much for us.

Rather than murder each other
we rented a second place
(Greta's house)

near the pool.
Now we are happily
duogamous.

There are ravens on the roof
of both places.
Perhaps they are the same ravens.

I can't tell.
If Roni Horn were here
she'd say ravens

are like water,
they are wildly constant.
They are a sign of Iceland.

I should learn more about signs.
I came to Stykkishólmur
to live in a library.

The library contains not books
but glaciers.
The glaciers are upright.

Silent.
As perfectly ordered as books would be.
But they are melted.

What would it be like
to live in a library
of melted books.

With sentences streaming over the floor
and all the punctuation
settled to the bottom as a residue.

It would be confusing.
Unforgivable.
A great adventure.

Roni Horn once told me
that one of the Antarctic explorers said
To be having an adventure

is a sign of incompetence.
When I am feeling
at my most incompetent

as I do in Stykkishólmur
many a dark morning
walking into the wind,

I try to conjure in mind
something that is the opposite of incompetence.
For example the egg.

This perfect form.
Perfect content.
Perfect food.

In your dreams
said a more recent explorer (Anna Freud)
you can have your eggs cooked as perfectly as you want

but you cannot eat them.
Sometimes at night
when I can't sleep

because of the wind
I go and stand
in the library of glaciers.

I stand in another world.
Not the past not the future.
Not paradise not reality not

a dream.
An *other* competence,
wild and constant.

Who knows why it exists.
I stand amid glaciers.
Listen to the wind outside

falling towards me from the outer edges of night and space.
I have no theory
of why we are here

or what any of us is a sign of.
But a room of melted glaciers
rocking in the nightwind of Stykkishólmur

is a good place to ponder it.
Each glacier is lit from underneath
as memory is.

Proust says memory is of two kinds.
There is the daily struggle to recall
where we put our reading glasses

and there is a deeper gust of longing
that comes up from the bottom
of the heart

involuntarily.
At sudden times.
For surprise reasons.

Here is an excerpt from a letter Proust wrote
in 1913:
We think we no longer love our dead

but that is because we do not remember them:
suddenly
we catch sight of an old glove

and burst into tears.
Before leaving the library
I turn off the lights.

The glaciers go dark.
Then I return to Greta's house.
Wake up my husband.

Ask him to make us some eggs.

from *London Review of Books*

Fidelity

◇　◇　◇

Fidelity, after long practice, to
The things that have crossed one's path in life,
Moves one to find "history" in a morning,
A moonlit night, a transitory patch
Of sun upon grass, the turning of a cat's
Sleek head over its shoulder to look back
Into one's eyes, a lifelong lover's touch,
The memory of the shy sweet sidelong
Smile of a friend one may not see again
In "this life"—these things define home
To one now that one lives largely in one's mind—
As though there had ever been any other
Place—once born, once having existed—
In which to somehow locate a world

Because brief hours before fadeout life becomes
A late awakening, much as one assumes
Is the experience of "lost" generations
Whose youth is turned back toward childhood by
Dreams; just so one's own dim youth now at last
Appears a kind of slumber from which the slow
Process of waking took a half century
Or so, as time now opens up its eyes,
Yawns, stretches, struggles in dark to discover
Where it is among whirling things, places, years.
But of course one will never fully emerge
From this fog, nor in one's heart wish to do so,
For mere excursions don't suffice on visits

To dead cities—excavation too's required,
Cries out the hungry unborn poem
Within us, demanding to exist *as*
If alive

from *Vanitas*

This Poem Had Better Be about the World We Actually Live In

◇ ◇ ◇

i. There's No Chance of a Proper Introduction to the World—

not given how we usually enter into it headfirst, crying
and pissing and, if not exactly stunned, then wide-eyed in the sudden light
and hungry most of all. Even before we know who we are, we call the world
by its first name, which not so surprisingly turns out to be
whatever we think we have coming. And doesn't that seem a little
unreasonably familiar, considering the formal, ages-old arrangement:
we take our small place here, already squirming; we have to vacate the premises
whenever the lease is up. We're signing on before we can manage even
two real words in a row, but hey—we know the world when we see it.
And when we say its name, we're so alive it hurts, already
wishing it could stay said that inchoate way forever.

ii. A Study Guide in Middle Age

There's no more relying on the first name of the world.
Now it goes by pseudonyms, aliases, guises and disguises, AKAs
for all occasions, schoolyard nicknames, epithets, and honorary titles.
And because there's no way you can hope to be encyclopedic,
here are just a few of those it wouldn't hurt to learn, remarkably
suitable in a variety of situations:

Fred. Kilroy. Ichabod. Cinquain-crazy Adelaide Crapsey.
Larson E. Whipsnade. The Little Tramp. Dewey, Cheatham, & Howe.

He who laughs last is slow to catch on. There will be a test on this.

Too Much with Us, Late and Soon. Late to Supper. Walk-ins Welcome.
God's Whoopee Cushion. The Runaway Train. All Hat and No Cattle.

You can know by heart more names for the world than anyone alive,
but you still can't take it with you.

Rough and Tumble. Wash & Wear. No Shoes, No Shirt, No Service.
Tiny Bubbles in the Wine. Sweet Beulah Land. Gone Fishing.

Any makeup exam will be significantly harder
than the one you should have been there for in the first place.

Blood on the Saddle. Money in the Bank. A Few Pickles Shy of a Barrel.
I Don't Know Art, but I Know What I Like.

Let's not mistake whatever isn't Hell for part of Heaven.

iii. Last Name Last

The world's last name is whatever we come up with when we leave it, ready
or not, even if no one else in the room can hear us—
if there is a room, if anybody else is hanging around.
It's the last thing we have to say, even if we can't quite speak it
out loud. It can't be as familiar as the world we were so sure of
having all the time in. The last name of the world is likely
something dusky, if not altogether dark. The last name of the world assuredly
is nothing that will have even once occurred to us before.
The last name of the world distinguishes it, finally,
as still the only place that can sustain the fragile likes of us
among so many scorched or frozen, far less habitable worlds.
The last name of the world is inescapable and, right now at least,

we can live with that—as long as we don't really know
what it means. The last name of the world will be unmistakably ours.

from *The Georgia Review*

An Individual History

◇　◇　◇

This was before the time of lithium and Zoloft

before mood stabilizers and anxiolytics

and almost all the psychotropic drugs, but not before thorazine,

which the suicide O'Laughlin called "handcuffs for the mind."

It was before, during, and after the time of atomic fallout,

Auschwitz, the Nakba, DDT, and you could take water cures,

find solace in quarantines, participate in shunnings,

or stand at Lourdes among the canes and crutches.

It was when the March of Time kept taking off its boots.

Fridays when families prayed the Living Rosary

to neutralize communists with prayer.

When electroshock was electrocution

and hammers recognized the purpose of a nail.

And so, if you were as crazy as my maternal grandmother was then

you might make the pilgrimage she did through the wards

of state and private institutions,

and make of your own body a nail for pounding, its head

sunk past quagmires, coups d'etat, and disappearances

and in this way find a place in history

among the detained and unparoled, an individual like her,

though hidden by an epoch of lean notation—"Marked

Parkinsonian tremor," "Chronic paranoid type"—

a time when the animal slowed by its fate

was excited to catch a glimpse of its tail

or feel through her skin the dulled-over joy

when for a moment her hands were still.

from *The Virginia Quarterly Review*

Grave

◇　◇　◇

What do you think of my new glasses
I asked as I stood under a shade tree
before the joined grave of my parents,

and what followed was a long silence
that descended on the rows of the dead
and on the fields and the woods beyond,

one of the one hundred kinds of silence
according to the Chinese belief,
each one distinct from the others,

but the differences being so faint
that only a few special monks
were able to tell one from another.

They make you look very scholarly,
I heard my mother say
once I lay down on the ground

and pressed an ear into the soft grass.
Then I rolled over and pressed
my other ear to the ground,

the ear my father likes to speak into,
but he would say nothing,
and I could not find a silence

among the one hundred Chinese silences
that would fit the one that he created
even though I was the one

who had just made up the business
of the one hundred Chinese silences—
the Silence of the Night Boat,

and the Silence of the Lotus,
cousin to the Silence of the Temple Bell
only deeper and softer, like petals, at its farthest edges.

from *The Atlantic*

Ugly Man

◇   ◇   ◇

Two months ago I found out I have a serious disease that's so rare it hasn't earned one of those nicknames like the flu. Even if I could pronounce its very long Latin name, the words would mean nothing. All you need to know is I'm being eaten alive by infections, and I'll be dead within three months if I'm lucky.

The worst side effect is a gradual, total destruction of my skin. It peels and flakes away in sheets. If I didn't spend half of my days in a tanning salon, I'd look like the moon. I'd have itched myself to death by now if my fingers weren't swollen into very painful, misshapen knobs.

When I was first diagnosed, my boyfriend said it didn't matter. But when there weren't enough porn DVDs in the world or a big enough increase in his allowance to give him an erection when we were in the same room, I cut him a final check and sent him on his way.

Now I buy prostitutes instead. It's obvious as soon as I undress they'll take no pleasure earning money from me. But they need the money just like I need to rub my husk against them. And I imagine they think that they've tasted worse and have been tasted by worse.

You don't know what it means to feel my chapped, disfigured lips and cock and hands saw away at something so downy. It's inexplicable. That's why it's hard for me to talk about the fact that my disease is so contagious a little peck on the cheek is enough to almost guarantee transmission.

In a few weeks, all the prostitutes I've hired will be the last boys on earth whom anyone would pay. Not long after I'm dead, they'll be dead.

Some nights I fantasize about telling them what saints they are, but I don't. Still, there are times when I almost get the feeling they know.

from *The Agriculture Reader*

KATE DANIELS

From "A Walk in Victoria's Secret"

◇   ◇   ◇

If an infant could speak, he would no doubt pronounce the act of sucking at his mother's breast by far the most important in his life.

S. Freud

I love smelly, sweaty breasts bound down in practical spandex to contract the
      orb's
circumference and inhibit unbalancing jiggling in order to win an Olympic
      Gold
or to swing, unimpeded, the number nine club on the eighteenth hole,
three under par, in the previously closed-to-women national Open . . .
And then there's the miracle of lactating breasts with their stretched nipples
and swollen globes of succulent flesh, the skin thinned at the sides,
raising the blue veins to the surface so it looks like a map.
I love breasts fastened into nursing bras with their flip-down
cups, facilitating a jutting-out as hilarious as coarse characters
in a Vegas strip show. I love the historical breasts of the milk nurse
who took up the noblewoman's babe and suckled it for wages.
And the furtively, thrust-through breasts, warming the iron bars
of the debtor's prison where the inmate took his comfort
from his mother or his wife. I love proletarian/ redneck/ sensible shoes/ 24–7/
workaday breasts, cheerfully spewing full-course meals or midnight snacks,
or fast food, drive-thru repasts while speeding down the interstate.
I love the milky nu-nu stuffed in the mouth to plug up the titty baby's untimely
      yowl.

★

Last night, I watched my sons on the O-line of the football field,
so distant in their grown up bodies, so far from mother's milk.
To remind them now of the meals they made of me would mortify
and unman them, so I keep that silence. Afterwards, I embraced them
in their helmets and their pads, and leaned hard into the rank,
erotic fragrance they emitted, yearning to return to our early years together,
when I was hardly more to them than a universe of approaching odor,
a twin-hulled, human spaceship rocketing across a galaxy
with my bursting, squirting cargo of warm, sweet milk . . .

★

I loved the smell inside my nursing bra. I used to dip my face inside,
and breathe, and pull away, feeling drunk solidarity with my hungry baby.

I loved the sodden *thunk* of soaked nursing pads flung to the floor.

I loved the oily, thin taste of my own milk.

I loved my husband's mouth, in the dark, relieving the pressure.

I loved the mounting. My baby mounting his objects of desire,
and making them run with milk, sucking out the cream,
raising the heat and falling back, drunk and gluttonous,
post-coital, on the sweaty, smelly pillow of my flesh.

Now that it's all over, now that my breasts are diminished and dried out
and will never run with milk again—

Now that my nipples are like those of a grammar school virgin,
and look like raisins desiccated past their prime—

Now that the specter of cancer of the breast is statistically more
than a distant possibility—
Now, that two empty bottles in the window above my writing desk,
once filled and refilled with Holman's Dairy milk, permanently
remind me of my former glory and gleam straight through
with absence I need only touch my chest to imagine—

Now I walk through the radiance of Victoria's Secret, drunk with the ghostly,
concave images of all those robust breasts, waiting to be suckled and cupped.

★

In her barely literate way, my mother's mother must have meditated
on the dual mysteries of every woman's breasts that Freud, in his genius,
almost ruined: the sweet delight of a baby's nursing, and the harder edges
of the pleasure delivered by a moaning lover's sucking mouth.
Far back in the previous century, I have conjured Victoria. I can
see her after supper, leaning over the dishpan in the kitchen sink, her mind
blessedly free of psychoanalysis. She pumps a basin full of cold, clear water,
and opens the front of her gingham dress, and lifts her beauties
from the thick white bindings of her homemade bra.
Leaning awkwardly, she dips them down and dabs them with a roughened,
dripping cloth. All day, her man has labored in the fields. In a corner
of their room, his dungarees crouch in crusted piles of stench as he falls,
        exhausted
on their bed. Even so, tunneling at the very edge of sleep, he moves towards
        her
for a tiny sip of sweetness, a sugary lozenge of buttery candy, he pulls into his
        mouth.
Now energy pulses him distantly, back in time, until he becomes
his very own, newborn baby. All's delightfully confused. Who is he now?
The child he put inside her belly two years back? Or his ancient, infant self
at ease upon the paradise of his mother's breast? And she, the phoenix nesting
on her bed of self-extinction, is sucked away deliciously. She's an object,
for the moment, experienced as subject: the breaking yolk of warmth between
        her legs,
the untidy buzzing rush of hormones in her head, the milk rising and rising,
breaking so exquisitely the unanalyzable mystery of flesh.

from *Women's Review of Books*

Four "Addresses"

◇   ◇   ◇

POEM ADDRESSING BOYS, AGE 5

This poem can turn invisible and it can beat up bad guys! When people read this poem it is like a laser shooting bad guys right in the stomach! This poem knocks bad guys on their bottoms! And if you need a force field you can get one from Dr. Defense who lives in this poem and makes a number of bad-guy-fighting tools and weapons. Sometimes giant robot bad guys try to kill this poem by bopping it on the head, but this poem doesn't allow that and sends ninjas and wizards out to reverse time and destroy the robots. Dr. Defense jumps up and kicks everyone in the face and he, like, flies through a window and then, like, this poem explodes!

POEM ADDRESSING PEOPLE WHO ARE TIRED, HUNGRY, OR HORNY

These things can wait. This is a very good poem and you'd be very myopic to lose sight of this beauty simply because some of your baser needs are asserting themselves. I'll keep this short, but you should exercise some control, okay? Stay with me here. Allow this poem to carry you beyond yourself, transcending your mortal flesh as you wed yourself with the potentially infinite.

POEM ADDRESSING PEOPLE WITH CERTAIN EXPECTATIONS ABOUT POETRY THAT ARE NOT FULFILLED IN THIS POEM

Change

POEM ADDRESSING PRISONERS

How this found you I don't know, but this is a good event, a good omen. Not because it's mystical or mysterious, but because you're actually reading this poem and I have actually written it. I know that this poem is a sort of prison too, but it's a much, much more beautiful one.

from *Double Room*

Come in from the Rain

◇　◇　◇

Stick that bumbershoot
in elephant's-foot

brolly stand behind
the big door. Mind

your manners at High Tea.
Hi, you. High ve-

locity hailstones cream
passersby beyond the panes. I dream

of Jeannie, starring Bar-
bara Eden, of Eden, star-

ring Eve and Adam, of Adam
Cartwright, a.k.a. the let-'em-

have-it-with-all-candor
Trapper John. Pander

to the mass-man mass-taste,
that's my motto. Waste

the day, the life, the villain
with depression, fill-in-

the-wrong-blanks misap-
prehension, dum-dums. Nap

an hour through the Buddy
Ebsen as a perspicacious fuddy-

duddy whodunit. Then produce
the silver teapot, loose

Earl Grey and table water
slabs. Somebody's daughter

carries on the grand tradition
in the grandma manner. Wishin'

you were here don't place you
in the old wing chair. Face you

in the photos, china, art
on parlor walls. It's raining in my heart.

from *Poetry*

Play

◇   ◇   ◇

I am on the outside now like my childless aunt
the one we all hated because my uncle doted on her

she didn't like children you could tell
and wore silk dresses that had to be dry-cleaned
how extravagant said my mother *she's spoiled* said the other aunts
who were busy in their polyester blends busy with their kids

I have a memory of this aunt eating bonbons
as I swung on a tire hung from a tree branch in her yard
my aunt didn't offer us any candy and that was just bad manners
even as a kindergartener I knew that

but now I have become that aunt
my sister-in-law wants my husband

to move in with her to take care of her children
and what do I know about suffering and divorces
and restraining orders what do I know about staying up all night
with a daughter with a fever

when I called about the $300 worth of extra cell phone charges
the woman at T-mobile said *honey I hate to be the one to tell you*
but there's a number and she read my sister-in-law's number
all the calls are to and from your husband's cell

sometimes they're on a couple of hours
they talked when I was at work

the woman said *I'm sorry* thinking my husband was having an affair
but the affair was with his sister and it wasn't an affair really
it was therapy and my husband was the therapist
even though he isn't a therapist

our niece wrote a one-act play in which a man is being abused
by his wife who is a witch a demon
and the man's kindly sister is trying to help him escape
I know you are being abused as I was once too the heroine says

my sister-in-law thought her brother was abused because he vacuumed once
I guess she thought he was doting on me
my husband thought he was abused because I asked him to cook dinner
when he didn't have a job for over a year

I understand why my aunt never fought back
because once you are labeled as someone terrible
there is nothing much you can do to change your reputation
there is no way to prove your kindness

if you are nice everyone will think you are phony trying to trick them
and if you are cold well it just confirms their theory

sometimes my husband disappears from this story
only to come back to say please *don't call my sister*
the other woman
it grosses me out

OK I won't

our niece got an A for her play
portraying me as ugly and cruel
and the teacher thought it was so realistic
her theater class even did a staged reading of it

a loud eighth-grade girl playing a shrill me
a small eighth-grade boy cowering as my husband

sometimes my uncle disappears from this story
only to come back

with a giant stuffed animal for me
and a kiss on the cheek for my aunt

when I stole two of her chocolates
and poked holes into the rest left in the box
she knew enough not to complain
and kept her squashed candies to herself

from *The Antioch Review*

Presidential Blackness

◇ ◇ ◇

[A Race Fearlessness Manifolk Destiny]

We miracles. We have not known true freedom in America or in Art, thus our work has struggled in containers not of our own construction; and yet, within those constraints, we have conjured a magnificent aesthetic toolbox, one that abolitions the flavor locked in foreign forms and second-hand technical devices. Boldly reaching into our own human-handbooks, we are widening—our hybrid, written surfaces exceeding genre and ism. Our vernacular-vision, the way we walk the talk and talk the walk, is its own page-lip-palette of lyric-fixins'. The Independence that once surrounded Nkrumah's head has finally reached us, saturation de conquer root, the motion of destiny!

1

The first footwork of Race Fearlessness is to fragment the linearity of the contemporary literary, color line. A black body, trained-in-the-tradition, can express a complete thought in as many movements as it has limbs, broken and healed. To prevent the community from lining up behind "A," "The," "I," or predictable proper nouns and pronouns, both moments of the march (the march-beginning and the march-end) must curve into each other like one of Bill Traylor's "self-taught" snakes of enjambment—the pictorial schema of black aesthetic, lyric progression.

2

To make an identity repair-kit of all of black folk behavior, to shine or show-off, as nuisance as nuance, sometimes some-timey and sometimes on-point, the slanguage of hood ornaments. Negritude, though often mistaken for primitivism, has made a comeback as the contemporary, commodity known as swagger. Hear me what I'm telling you: in addition to being solidarity to brothers in prison, blue jeans worn hanging off the body also mean Kiss our Black ass.

3

As it is not possible to "purely" disagree in English, or, for African descendants, to "truly" agree with England, Race Fearlessness is committed to subject-verb disagreement, its liberating conflict. Yes there are forms of literacy and illiteracy both capable of innovative-revolution, of continuing our collective inner face. A new infinite alphabet pours from the pores of the poor.

4

If we close the door and write "Colored Only" on it or "No Whites Allowed," it is not out of Cult-Nats Conceptualism. The only segregation we desire is segregation by choice, a segre-gathering of abundant healing, neither separatism or ghetto-fetish. If we are successful, we will emerge from behind that door capable of forgiving our former owners for cultivating more tokens than allies of color.

5

Our heroic run, back and forth, between "invisibility" and "mask," North and South, and "I" and "We," has strengthened (though fragmented) our consciousness. To bid ourselves a legacy of reference-pride, we are worrying all allusions to Greek Mythology (especially Persephone) back into their worn, believe- and make-believe exiles, their bad pale labors. It's time for a new passage; one minus the triangular, choir-less, trade of great-great-great-grand slaves, one that signifies.

Our Negro Heroico is not one of Renaissance or Power or Cutting Edge or Hype or Post Anything. We did not arrive after us, not after Race not after Blackness. Taught long ago to separate "what white folks done to us" from "what we got to do for us," we are no longer hurt in the world, were not hurt into art, and are not above hurting those who continue to take advantage of and hurt the babymuva of civilization, Africa. We seek wholeness—not competition, completion—to be rejoined with our many sold-off selves. Equator, belt of civilization, you are our breathing line, the vein of Ra. We seek a Presidential Blackness, ready to break the mouth of tomorrow, Now.

from *The Oxford American*

Dear Final Journey,

◇　◇　◇

Dear Noose, Dear Necktie, Dear Cravat,
Salutations, big ship, toiling the dark waters
Of death. Dear Freighter, in whose hold the oily links
Of the anchor's chain, like snakes, are coiled. Dear Oily
Waters, salve and balm, black disk of ocean across which,
Dark Craft, you creak, loom, until your black gobbles
The horizon up. Dear black firmament and earth,
Ditch of the kicked in. World shut and over,
Mingy and dim. Dear Line, Dear Sinker,
Noose and Hook,

Hello.

from *Boston Review*

What Is It about Hands?

◇   ◇   ◇

1.

I never think of them.

They do their work automatically.

Mine are small and childish—almost paws.

I'm not "good with them."

Once when I was young, my mother burst out laughing
as she watched me try to sew a hem.

2.

Wait, now it comes back to me—

my obsession with hands—not real ones,

but the hands of statues and mannequins
with their perfect fingers and polished nails.

They seemed to reach out—
"a spare pair" from another world
offering metaphysical assistance.

I bought one from a street vendor
who had a whole array of artificial limbs
spread out on a blanket.

How I loved that hand! Would hold it shyly
when alone—and kept it on my coffee table
to add a surreal touch.

But some girls I worked with came over for drinks
and stole it. I remember calling them and feeling rather silly saying:
"I know you've got my hand and I want it back."

Them giggling, then finally acquiescing.
It wasn't the same though. I looked at it differently—
not knowing where it had been.

from *LIT*

Apologia

◇ ◇ ◇

*However innocent your life may have been, no Chris-
tian ought to venture to die in any other state than that
of the penitent.*

—Saint Augustine

I have been sodden with wine.
I have been confused by wine.
I have been lied to by men,
And yet, I lie down upon such men,
Still and willing in the manners that they please.
Lord, I've been the blemish at your love feast.

And I've been tangled in nettles and brambles,
Have dwelt in seamy hotels, have ambled
Down roads that once, so necessary,
Seemed. And I've prayed, hot and overloadedly,
Having meddled in such matters
That ought be closed to me.

Darkness, I have done dread deeds in,
Hearkening to apocalyptic heathen,
Even as I cocked my lips to yours. And I have slept
On floors. And I have crept along on all fours.
And. *More.* I have lived briskly in nice houses.
I have swigged whiskey in icehouses.

I have been June, July, and August.
I have been riotous when I felt like I must
Or I could be. And I've hung on your tree like a ripe fig

Desiring to be plucked. And I've flung my body to your bed
Like a white bride pining to be rubbed up against.
Like a suckling child hungry in a viper's den.

And I have been Dismas, the penitent
Thief. And I have been Judas. And I've spent
My plenty silvers chiefly on my hells.
In that, I have seldom, if ever, failed.
It's just as well. For as the ibis devours her carrion,
I feed upon what queasy defeats I carry on

My back. Thus the beggar becomes her bowl.
And the hangwoman surrenders to the scaffold.
And irrevocable acts of god and doom consume me.
Can this be mercy? I fear there isn't any
Left. Even the chrism is bereft.
Wretched, most wretched it says,

While my guilt unfolds like a napkin in your lap.
Will a dog grow fat on crumbs the master drops?
I have been a grabber at your garment hem.
And I have been a Magdalene outside your tomb.
And I've bathed atop roofs, have pounded with rue,
Have pooled my pearls, the sorrowful few—

Like milky mea culpas they rattle fragile on a string.
Christ: Forgive me *everything*.

from *Image*

B . H . F A I R C H I L D

On the Waterfront

◇　◇　◇

—Know thyself

Flashlight in hand, I stand just inside the door
in my starched white shirt, red jacket nailed shut
by six gold buttons, and a plastic black bow tie,
a sort of smaller movie screen reflecting back
the larger one. *Is that really you?* says Mrs. Pierce,
my Latin teacher, as I lead her to her seat
between the Neiderlands, our neighbors, and Mickey Breen,
who owns the liquor store. Walking back, I see
their faces bright and childlike in the mirrored glare
of a hard winter New York sky. I know them all,
these small-town worried faces, these natives of the known,
the real, a highway and brown fields; and New York
is a foreign land—the waterfront, unions, priests,
the tugboat's moan—exotic as Siam or Casablanca.
I have seen this movie seven times, memorized the lines:
Edie, raised by nuns, pleading—praying really—
Isn't everyone a part of everybody else?
and Terry, angry, stunned with guilt, *Quit worrying*
about the truth. Worry about yourself, while I,
in this one-movie Kansas town where everyone
is a part of everybody else, am waiting darkly
for a self to worry over, a name, a place,
New York, on 52nd Street between the Five Spot
and Jimmy Ryan's where bebop and blue neon lights
would fill my room, and I would wear a porkpie hat
and play tenor saxophone like Lester Young, but now,
however, I am lost, and Edie, too, and Charlie,

Father Barry, Pop, even Terry because he worried
more about the truth than he did about himself,
and I scan the little mounds of bodies now lost even
to themselves as the movie rushes to its end,
car lights winging down an alley, quick shadows
fluttering across this East River of familiar faces
like storm clouds cluttering a wheat field or geese
in autumn plowing through the sun, that honking,
that moan of a boat in fog. I walk outside
to cop a smoke, *I could have been a contender,*
I could have been somebody instead of who I am,
and look across the street at the Army-Navy store
where we would try on gas masks, and Elmer Fox
would let us hold the Purple Hearts, but it's over now,
and they are leaving, *Goodnight, Mr. Neiderland,*
Goodnight, Mrs. Neiderland, Goodnight, Mick, Goodnight,
Mrs. Pierce, as she, a woman who has lived alone
for forty years and for two of those has suffered through
my botched translations from the Latin tongue, smiles,
Nosce te ipsum, and I have no idea what she means.

from *Sewanee Review*

VIEVEE FRANCIS

Smoke under the Bale

◇　◇　◇

My story—hieroglyphics of scuff and blister.
How can you know me? Tin and bridle,
neigh and crocker sack. My gandy-song—
the blue-buzz of flies.
Sugar from your palm? No.
Give me your fingers. Under this hairshirt
steams the vocabulary of the flesh,
crosshatched and scarred into meaning.

from *Callaloo*

At the River

◊   ◊   ◊

One night that summer my mother decided it was time to tell me about
what she referred to as *pleasure,* though you could see she felt
some sort of unease about this ceremony, which she tried to cover up
by first taking my hand, as though somebody in the family had just died—
she went on holding my hand as she made her speech
which was more like a speech about mechanical engineering
than a conversation about pleasure. In her other hand
she had a book from which, apparently, she'd taken the main facts.
She did the same thing with the others, my two brothers and sister,
and the book was always the same book, dark blue,
though we each got our own copy.

There was a line drawing on the cover
showing a man and woman holding hands
but standing fairly far apart, like people on two sides of a dirt road.

Obviously, she and my father did not have a language for what they did
which, from what I could judge, wasn't pleasure.
At the same time, whatever holds human beings together
could hardly resemble those cool black-and-white diagrams, which suggested,
among other things, that you could only achieve pleasure
with a person of the opposite sex,
so you didn't get two sockets, say, and no plug.

School wasn't in session.
I went back to my room and shut the door
and my mother went into the kitchen
where my father was pouring glasses of wine for himself and his invisible guest
who—surprise—doesn't appear.

No, it's just my father and his friend the Holy Ghost
partying the night away until the bottle runs out,
after which my father continues sitting at the table
with an open book in front of him.

Tactfully, so as not to embarrass the Spirit,
my father handled all the glasses,
first his own, then the other, back and forth like every other night.

By then, I was out of the house.
It was summer; my friends used to meet at the river.
The whole thing seemed a grave embarrassment
although the truth was that, except for the boys, maybe we didn't understand
                    mechanics.
The boys had the key right in front of them, in their hands if they wanted,
and many of them said they'd already used it,
though once one boy said this, the others said it too,
and of course people had older brothers and sisters.

We sat at the edge of the river discussing parents in general
and sex in particular. And a lot of information got shared,
and of course the subject was unfailingly interesting.
I showed people my book, *Ideal Marriage*—we all had a good laugh over it.
One night a boy brought a bottle of wine and we passed it around for a while.

More and more that summer we understood
that something was going to happen to us
that would change us.
And the group, all of us who used to meet this way,
the group would shatter, like a shell that falls away
so the bird can emerge.
Only of course it would be two birds emerging, pairs of birds.

We sat in the reeds at the edge of the river
throwing small stones. When the stones hit,
you could see the stars multiply for a second, little explosions of light
flashing and going out. There was a boy I was beginning to like,
not to speak to but to watch.
I liked to sit behind him to study the back of his neck.

And after a while we'd all get up together and walk back through the dark
to the village. Above the field, the sky was clear,
stars everywhere, like in the river, though these were the real stars,
even the dead ones were real.

But the ones in the river—
they were like having some idea that explodes suddenly into a thousand ideas,
not real, maybe, but somehow more lifelike.

When I got home, my mother was asleep, my father was still at the table,
reading his book. And I said, Did your friend go away?
And he looked at me intently for a while,
then he said, Your mother and I used to drink a glass of wine together
after dinner.

from *The New Yorker*

What's Left

◇   ◇   ◇

Each was so exalted in the presence of the other
(those two newlyweds, or maybe weekend lovers,
in a booth at the diner they shared exuberance
lifted into the feel of a garden nook
in a Renaissance painting of Eden) that their feeding
one another from an order of eggs and cheezie tots
exuded something both sexual and inexplicably
sacred at once. They left two minutes ago;
already what's left is a smear of hardening yolk,
a curl of grease going rancid, and emptiness
—or worse, Shel thinks, than emptiness:
abandonment. She clears the table. Her job
now is to erase all trace that they were here.
And she thinks that this might be—the yolk,
the jelling grease—what everything is, and everyone,
remaining from when Preexistence exploded
the Universe out of itself, and that unformed
and ultraradiant promise settled into the laws
of thermodynamics and the alleys of evolution;
and light-without-taint and energy unconfined
awoke the next morning and segued into
the first of the pissy squabbles and the small
betrayals that matter-rallied-into-human-consciousness
finds unavoidable: someone leaves
a telltale receipt on the kitchen counter, someone
leaves a text messaging account
in the open air. When the angels
finally took leave of Abraham's tent, the three
who arrived disguised as ragged travelers and then,

confronted by his hospitality, opened their cloaks
so the flow of a higher order of being
silverplated the cloth walls and provided
an on-loan bounty and calm . . . when they departed,
what remained but a few bedraggled feathers
on the hard-tamped sand, like any confetti
the sweepers contend with after the parade.
And that's our story, she thinks, our story today:
the gods no longer walk around our world
in a believable way, and we're left here
with the crusts, the rinds, the lees,
the weekly paycheck and the boss who brushes
up against her pillowy ass too regularly
for chance. But what *do* we want?
—to revert to those fictions, inventing
a deity only so it can then invent us?
It's hard to know *what* to think: and luckily,
now she *doesn't* have to think: her hands
instinctively take over. While her brain
revolves in blitzspace, one by one the plates
slip into the sudsy water, and out, and gleam
like the sign of a covenant, a functional peace,
that she's made with the one life she has.

from *Boulevard*

Namaskar

◇   ◇   ◇

Intimate strangers, each of us is bent
On bending the other to our will. But will
We ever understand what's really meant
By entering into this argument
Together? There's no lesson to instill

In this place, even if our subject matter's
The worthy cause of coming to a higher
Knowledge of self. (The self's the thing that natters
So ceaselessly inside of you, it shatters
Any nascent scintilla of desire

To know it better.) Going to the mat
Assumes an almost mythic context just
The same. Yoga means *union*. Yet the spat
Revives with every lesson for all that.
Body and mind: complete breakdown of trust,

Supremacy of superego, limbs
And limbic system bickering on and on
About whose fault the pain is. Practice skims
That surface racket; postural synonyms
Outline a body-language lexicon

That's liminal, phoned-in. Here we are all
Posers, and maybe posturing is part
And parcel of a process we don't call

By its right name anyway. But if we fall
Flat on our asanas, that's all right: the art

Of falling's still an art. Cold feet can be
Adaptive, even in the stifling heat
Of this room. Flesh and intention finally
Wedded: bliss. Or should be. But do we
Not all resist change? This is the conceit

These postures mean to teach, a metaphor
That operates in every cell. Arranged
Marriage is not a custom we explore
Willingly in this culture, and the more
Uncomfortable we are, the more estranged

We feel: the hour-long meltdown's just enough
To heighten, rather than disrupt, our trust
In body-mind duality, a bluff
We've bought for centuries. Union is tough,
The more so if you absolutely must

Task yourself with believing that you chose
Your partner knowingly. Better to see
We're all stuck here with strangers, and who knows
What skeletons are underneath the clothes
In all our closets? Did I want to be

This tough, or this resilient? I had thought
I did. But physics isn't my strong suit
And never was. Tied roughly in a knot
To contemplate dynamic tension, hot
Under the collarbone, there's an acute

Desire to flee: if I could figure out
How to support myself apart from you,
Dear body, I'd be out of here without
A thought. But then, one last breath, and all doubt
Disperses, and we feel just for a few

Seconds how it would feel to understand
For real the truth that practice does not make
Perfect: it is perfect. And we land
Upright, and hand rests folio-like on hand,
Something about to open for its own sake.

from *Sewanee Theological Review*

Passing the Barnyard Graveyard

◇   ◇   ◇

I sang Elvis to the shorn sheep,
and they didn't run away.
I sang Patsy to the fine ass
who chewed crabgrass and brayed.
I sang Bonnie to the bunny:
mini, milk-eyed, and gray.
I sang Johnny to the Billy goat.
He could have listened all day.
I sang Piaf to the gravestones:
Fantômes, parlez vous Français?

from *The Antioch Review*

Oh dont

◇   ◇   ◇

—Albumen silver print attributed to F. M. Parkes & Reeves

the spirit wrote
after the Civil War,
in cloudy script
like you might expect
from someone without
hands, the mediums
busy with so many dead,
collective push
into the other world,
all of us calling.
Down by the river
I remembered sawdust,
his guitar, two or three
songs, his hand palm
up, showing me the place
where his mother died,
like a mirror he thought
of his own death, and when
the table turned,
he appeared. We walked
around a fallen tree,
the woman in me still
driving by. His dance
was the best part, I mean
no one was dancing, men
and women in night
outfits. Even broken,

cement to my thigh,
I climbed the stairs
and breathed the way
I did at fifteen, taking
in the burning. One spirit
passed her arm through
a chair, roses, like the ones
he carried to me saying
he'd never sleep again.
There's red in the sky, red
in the table, like winter,
the shining garment that materialized.
Oh dont keep calling?
Oh dont stop?
In another photograph,
a spirit has written *Difficult*
to manifest present conditions
not suitable, and another, in tiny
script, *la porte ferme*—so hard
to see it could be *fume,* though
the closed door is what I've stared
at so long, when even
a blind girl can see that's smoke.

from *Witness*

And What, Friends,
Is Called a Road?

◇   ◇   ◇

And what, friends, is called a road? If there is, friends, an island, akin to a river, resembling a fence, used in the purpose of swiftly moving bodies and goods, a hallway lined in names, an aisle through counties, a duct in webs, a gangway to seeds, a traveling of beings, a river composed of islands, a place of simultaneous attraction and repulsion, a place for the finding of place, an area of exchange like unto an immense abacus. This, friends, is called a road.

And what, friends, is a car? If there is, friends, a metal corpuscle, a small room in which one cannot walk, a kind of peregrine room, a metal corpuscle battened to wheels, with an interior fitted with instruments used to control its movement, purposed to haul bodies from place to place with minimal exertion on the musculature of those bodies, being thus a small room on wheels that metallizes the human body, being a small mobilized building, a portable shack, conveying of hairdos, children, coins, drinks and fuels across the air and into the surface of hills and athwart old and dull and glittering rivers. This, friends, is called a car.

And what, friends, is called a daughter? If there is, friends, a little girl, impressionable, precious, complex, in need of love, desiring of security, warmth, kindness, giving of kindness, who is brave, who witnesses storms in awe and in fright, who enjoys big trees, has seen the fighting of her parents, owns a teddybear, goes with a teddybear, carries a white stuffed polar bear throughout her childhood, who is five, who is six, who is nine, who makes little camps in livingrooms, or in the backs of great cars, who is as an enfoldment of joy and whose life, despite her parents' efforts, is still surrounded by the causes of death, who is ten, who still finds grief, whose small hands are growing away, whose large eyes are growing away, whose funny way of talking is growing away. This, friends, is called a daughter.

And what, for us, is called a long-distance relationship? If there are friends, or any two people separated purposefully by a distance, whose history of interaction is characterized by misunderstanding, frequent fighting and interpersonal pain, such that the factors of their differences of age, culture, their styles of temperament and the scripts they were taught (in which they may seem imprisoned) have exercised them to a distance, of say eleven hundred miles, and who, despite compatibilities, and because of incompatibilities, find themselves frustrated yet willing to try. This, friends, is called a long-distance relationship.

And what, at last, is called a notebook? If, friends, there is a road through emptiness, a sea sewn to a spine, placed on tables, laps, or on the passenger seat of a car, used for palliation in a wash of disappearances, in haphazard recording of minutiae, road conditions, the recording of road condition and aggregates of thought that occur while driving on a condition, the invitation of emotion and radio, the notation of sign, a setting down of compendious or incidental note, in the grammars of back and forth going, the traveling from period to period, the coming from west to west, a sending between, a going in weather, whether between Illinois and Rhode Island, whether Normal and Providence, or between any several places normal, providential, for the purposes of trying to be happy, or of saving one's relationship, with one's estranged partner, or of seeing one's small daughter, during a separation, or of seeing her during a divorce, or of seeing her, during her swift youth after a divorce, or of driving to participate, even briefly, in the life of a sadder and less buoyant daughter, a little daughter, who is brave, who puts her chin up, who is kind, who only wishes to be happy, whom one cannot find a job near, for the recording of any elemental time of alienation, for the chronicling of any emotional pain, evoked by any unnatural distance, from a small daughter, one might love, with all one's understanding, such that, by a collection of scrawl, in an accrual of insight, some use be invited, to recollect painful things, that they may not become misery, and the refusal, to be steered by pain, or to recollect, and in fact insist, the living, with awareness, to joy, to recollect this way, for a daughter, when she is grown, or for oneself, or for anyone else, who may have found, to whatever degree, in this place of orphans, this endless humility, in our sorrow for lost homes. This, friends, is called a notebook.

from *Action Yes Online Quarterly*

The Poetic Memoirs of Lady Daibu

◇ ◇ ◇

That morning, to research the form,
she rummaged in a crawlspace for a volume
her father had lent a dozen years before.
He no longer speaks to her—
her poems referring to him
are venomous, he claims—
though he does reminisce with her children and ex
on the years she was an infant
when friends still dropped by early evenings for a drink.
That afternoon,

inside the cover of Lady Daibu's memoir
she found a few notes in his scrawl:
hitori sumire, a single violet,
contains the phrase
> *hitori sumi,*
>> *living alone*

And because he does not live with her mother
perhaps these notes to himself
stay to himself and journal entries:

> *the cricket's loud confusion*

> *moon's tranquil brightness*

Did he know their correspondence would come to this—
scraps of allusions tucked between pages?
This morning,

when she opens the memoir,
she cannot tell which are her father's underlined passages
and which are her own—
for the one to whom I wanted to show it was not there—
seeing how a language so poor in vocabulary
can be so rife with ambiguity.

from *Court Green*

Five "Lingo Sonnets"

◇ ◇ ◇

CALIBAN PASSES HIS DRIVING TEST ON THE NINTH TRY

Can I tell you a secret? Parallel parking was nothing. I could
even fake the hand signals most of the time—well, maybe half.
Going straight was my bête noir. Give me a freeway and crash!
I was driving back from a weekend gambling in Atlantic City, N.J.,
keester strapped tight, following all the rules, when the wheel
made a mad dash for freedom. I can drive any road on any mountain,
only one hand, but a straightaway turns me into Mr. Twitchy. Keep
quiet about it, will ya? I'm trying to get a chauffeur's license. Four
sevens and I took home twenty grand. I gave the cop a ten spot
under the neon Seven-Eleven sign near Exit 282. The *E* and *V*
were on the blink, sputtering like Prospero when his little minx
yelled *Rape*. All I wanted from the drip was a simple waltz
around the campsite, a kiss. Sheesh—women! Hey, watch that curb!

DESDEMONA RESUSCITATED BY SIR JOHN FALSTAFF, EMT

Doppelgänger or damsel in distress, it was all one to me
from the first time I checked her lily-white pulse—heading
horizontal. So I figure I'll try the breath of life. Gadzooks! I
just made it, her chest rising hard as a horse's kick,
like a battlefield cannon. Don't get me wrong. I'm
no miracle worker, but I know a thing or two about pulses, so
press the chest hard—the heart is buried deep. You can't rescue
Rapunzel from the tower with a limp handshake. As

the blood starts pumping, you see it in the cheeks first. You
vow to drink less every time you lose one, then drink more. Wow,
X-rays are crazy, man. Last week a guy swallowed a gas cap. Why?
Zounds! Who knows? Maybe he had a slow leak inside, a
butane fire in his gut. Zeus! That could make a snowman panic.

GANYMEDE'S DREAM OF ROSALIND

Girlfriend, I am the boyfriend you never had—honeysuckle mouth,
indigent eyes, no rough Barbary beard when kissing me. Popinjay,
keep me in your little chest, nestle me in your cosy love hotel,
my mouthful of tangy violets, my pumpkin raviolo, my spoon
of crushed moonlight in June. On your breast let me sup,
quaff the nectar of your sweet quim, trim repository of dear
succulence. Only touch my cheek with your hand, and let
us again meet as we did that first time in Act II, Scene IV
when we ran away to the Forest of Arden. Rough sphinx,
you know my heart, because it's yours, too, and quartz,
altogether transparent stone. I yearn for you as a crab
craves the wet sand, a wildebeest the vast savannah, a toad
every mudhole and mossy shelf. Forget Orlando. I'll marry myself.

I FIND AN ENTRANCE TO HELL

I'm with my mother in the Social Security office in Honolulu, and Karen J.
Kapenski is sitting across the desk telling this 80-year-old woman she'll
make no money from my father's death, like she lived in that prison
over fifty years for a check every month, and worse than that particular poop,
Queen Karen reveals Ronald Reagan is responsible, which is a bugger
since Mom voted for him both times. On the wall is a portrait of the current
Undersecretary of Satan and his grand vizier, a skinny bully and his heavy,
with vice-Satan's head sunk into his chest like melted beeswax,
Young Worthless with his simp's smirk, and I think, What a phiz,
and I know she's going to vote for them again. There's a proverb,
cheesy but apropos, lurking in here somewhere, but I'm as dead as my dad,
easygoing deacon & ladies' man, who never thought of anyone but himself.
"God has him now," Mom says, but here are the numbers. You do the math.

No, no, no, no—he doesn't even have nerves of steel. No
point asking him to save you, ma'am, he's more likely to rescue
rain from the street. Born on your block, not Krypton, he's
terror with a capital "T," the beautiful mind you
vain dames can't see for the mascara on your lashes. You saw
exactly nothing when you clapped eyes on him, a nerdy
zip, not even head of the class, just skulking in the back, a
brilliant light in a room full of blind men. But when he rises, havoc
descends on the world, lightning storms blister the earth, for he
fears nothing, feels nothing, sees everything. From the beginning
he's been a juggernaut, crushing everything in his path, from the Hindi
Jagannath, Lord of the World, a guise of the god Vishnu. A dark
Lex Luthor was more what I was thinking of than Superman, ma'am.

from *Verse*

I Just Want to Look

◊   ◊   ◊

A friend called to tell me there was a topless woman picketing
outside the courthouse so I got my keys and eyeglasses,
but when I got there, there were already so many onlookers,
I could see nothing but the top of her sign reading:
I HAVE THE RIGHT TO—the rest of it was blocked
by bobble-headed men in suits, by near boys in ball caps,
by afros and bald spots. "What does it say?" I asked the mail
man fanning himself with a big confidential-looking envelope.
"I'm sorry," he said, then, "Is this for you?" handing me
an envelope which had nothing but "To son" "From Mom"
written on it. The crowd moved a foot or two east, then
a foot or two west following the bare sign-bearing woman.
"I know I should have given it to you long ago," the mailman
was saying, "but I just couldn't bear being the bearer of bad news
another day." "That's what you think," a large woman yelled down
in the direction of the topless woman from the second floor
of the courthouse, tossing out what looked like an old jacket.
The men sent a disapproving roar up and the jacket seemed
to gather wind and flap off toward the river. "You have no idea
how hard my job is," the mailman said below the ruckus.
Something was going on at the steps of the courthouse.
"Is she dressing now," I asked a policeman fondling his nightstick.
"You're lucky," he said and I thought maybe he knew how I'd stopped
less than an inch from the kneecaps of an old lady pedestrian
that morning. "Your name is Lucky Jefferson, correct?
The infamous numbers runner and star pimp of Garfield?"
"No, no, I don't know what you're talking about," I said,
"And there is never anything in my own mailbox," the mailman
Sobbed to me. It was like a dark forest there in the middle

of downtown, all that shoulder to shouldering and gawking
at backs. The policeman stared at me and said, "I'm sure
you're Lucky. We were in high school together. Remember the night
we listened to *Purple Rain* until my mother got home
from her job at the hospital?" "Rick," I said. "Is that you?
Lord, I never thought you'd become a cop!" "My name is Alvin,"
the policeman said reaching for his cuffs. Inside the envelope
the mailman gave me I found a drawing of daisies in a blue vase
and below them the words: *You forgot Mother's Day, Bastard.*
"Woooo!" the crowd said, but I still could see nothing
of the topless woman. "I send my mother cards, but she sends nothing
to me," the mailman said. The policeman lay a hand on his shoulder.
The woman from the second floor of the courthouse yelled,
"No, no you don't have the right to do that!" and I realized suddenly
she was talking to me. I lifted the empty envelope over my head
and I swear everyone in the crowd turned to face me.

from *MiPOesias*

The Cunning Optimism of Language

◇ ◇ ◇

She made me Overlord of the Sewers.
It was a quiet ceremony before bed, consisting of,
you are Overlord of the Sewers. I'm unsure
what my powers are, though clearly absolute,
I thought as we kissed good night. Waking
in this state, I found coffee tasted the same.
I've left a note to my underlings: make
everything better. I'm particularly curious
about raisin bread. How can raisin bread
be improved? Not the cheap shit
but the good stuff. This is love, I tell you,
the random bestowal of a title. Anything else
is fraudulent. Now you have something, sort of
like a tag, by which to gauge if your love is real.
As our beds will tell you, do not remove the tag
under penalty of law. Such stern cops, our beds.
Go to sleep, they tell us, make love, they tell us,
die. If your lover makes you Overlord, don't ask,
of what? These are one-time offers, I fear,
just as the lightbulb that burned out
last night gets one chance to fail.
I have these minutes, all these chances to fail,
I must be many lightbulbs. It's well-lit
except in the corners, this life.

from *Conduit*

North Alabama Endtime

◇　◇　◇

Earlie has come to my house
on Sunday in a Chevy Nova
to say that the world is ending.
"Anyone can see it," he says.
"The signs are right before us,
your global warming,
your famine and pestilence,
your jihads and holy wars."

"I don't know," I say to Earlie.
"Maybe the physics guys see it—
quarks, muons, neutrinos—
the building blocks of matter
are naked as pole dancers
to those geniuses, but us,
we read but we're ignorant.
We're like goats eating paper."

"No, it's scripture," says Earlie.
"It's right there in Revelations.
The world is going to end.
You've hardened your heart."
"People are going to cry," says
Earlie's oldest boy, Tabor,
and looks straight at me,
"for the rocks to fall on them."

"I can nearly see that," I tell Tabor.
"People get depressed. It seems
like there's no way out, but then,
maybe they let it go a day,
something fantastic happens,
they change prescriptions
a redhead moves to town—
Yesterday I saved a turtle's life."

"You're too negative about
the end of time," says Earlie.
"It's like anything different.
You have to give it a chance,
strike while the iron is hot.
And it's hot, it's very hot.
The battle of Armageddon
has probably already started."

"I'd like to be more positive,"
I say. "And I try. I really do.
I read all I can about wars,
and the evil in men's hearts
but it's tough with the end.
It's like the championship,
Nothing is playing Infinity.
It looks to me like a dead tie."

"You're wrong," says Tabor,
"Good triumphs in the end."
"He's got you there," says Earlie,
"Good always whips evil's ass.
Just wait. People are going
to weep and gnash their teeth.
Not that you will," he says.
"You're thinking. That's a start."

"I hope it's not too late," I say,
and wave as they drive off,
not bad men, disturbed maybe,

but like all Turrentines, friendly.
You can say anything to them.
Probably they just got carried away.
They meant to talk politics.
The end of time was just a pretext.

from *Five Points*

MICHAELA KAHN

If I ring my body like a bell of coins, will the shock waves of that sound cause oil rigs & volcanoes to erupt?

◇　◇　◇

1.

If the praying mantis who lived in our kitchen for 17 days really did rise from the grave where we buried her (all that was left next day, an empty hole between basil and oregano) and fly to some other home, other rice field, perhaps the weapons of war will fold like chrysanthemums under their own weight, the notion of war collapse like matter inside the sun.

2.

Two more days of bombing in Afghanistan; egrets fly low over the rice fields. A woman loses four children beneath the rubble of a house; the central valley smells of smoke. Most symptoms only hint at the larger truth. The rest lies hidden beneath a stone, buried in a garden somewhere . . .

3.

Belgium. What was buried: a bottle of Cognac (hidden from the now retreating Nazis) given to a GI for promising to locate the Belgian's son. What seals this promise is an exchange of crucifixes between the men.

What is buried are ashes—a shoebox full of photographs taken when the GI and his small group came upon an abandoned concentration camp. He buries them beneath the backyard fig tree, but is not able to burn the afterimages of skeletons and ash from his mind. (And when his daughter marries a Jew, can't forgive his son-in-law.)

4.

This same story played out 5,000 years ago in the crab river-mud where a woman sang songs as she washed her clothes and her husband, miles away, was slain by sword in a battle for possession of that river.

(What is left, the hollow of her palm print in clay—hanging in a museum.)

5.

My mother told me if you bury something in the backyard, a toy truck or a small metal soldier, you will not find it there two weeks later. She said the sand is always moving, cycling—that the stone you find near the fig tree is from China or Istanbul. That the toy soldier will reappear 50 years later, slightly wet, salty.

6.

When he is many years dead, the GI's granddaughter (half-Catholic/ half-Jew) holds the Belgian crucifix with shaky fingers, turns the pin at the bottom, opens it, finds the smell of rain wafting up from the relic toenail inside.

from *Sentence*

Rome

◇　◇　◇

I saw once, in a rose garden, a remarkable statue of the Roman she-wolf
and her twins, a reproduction of an ancient statue—not the famous
bronze statue, so often copied, in which the wolf's blunt head swings
forward toward the viewer like a sad battering ram, but an even older
statue, of provenance less clear. The wolf had been cut out of black
stone, made blacker by the garden's shadows, and she stood in profile,
her elegant head pointed toward something far beyond her, her long
unmarked body and legs—narrower and more finely boned than the
body and legs of wolves as we know them—possessed, it seemed, of a
great stillness, like the saturated stillness of the roses, but tightly nerved,
set, on the instant, to move. Under her belly, stood the boys, under
her black breasts, not babes, as one might expect, but two lean boys,
cut from the same shadowed stone as the wolf, but disproportionately
small, grown boys no bigger than starlings, though still, like the wolf,
oddly fine of face and limb, one boy pressing four fingers against one
long breast, his other hand cupped beneath it to catch the falling milk,
the second boy wrapping both arms around another breast, as if to carry
it off, neither boy suckling, both instead turned toward you, dreamy,
sweetly sly, as if to chide you for interrupting their feeding, or as if they
were plotting a good trick . . . Beautiful, those boys among the roses.
Beautiful, the black wolf. But it was the breasts that held the eye, a
double row of four black breasts, eight smooth breasts, each narrowing
to a strict point, piercing sharp, exactly the shape of the ivory tooth of
the shark.

from *Ploughshares*

Six from "Birds of Self-Knowledge"

◇　◇　◇

BOBOLINK OF SCIENCE MUSEUMS

ancient maps	of the world
featured sea	monsters
wax models	of fetuses
in wombs	beware
a holy whore	the equation
of look	and lack
Shelley's heart	did not burn
in the funeral	pyre
so we kept it	for millennia
wrapped	in paper

TANAGER OF CARAPACE

command these maidservants
to fulfill duties
of the kushti　　　　rites
we sell fish cassava kola nuts
by the roadside
give birth to children
of soldier　　　　rapists
in the forests　　　solace
solely in dining
on old velvet

                    pullets
        so: we find
    some aardvarks
        ! who fall in love with us !
        then we are happy

HAWK OF MOONSTONES

afterthreenightswithoutsleepIcatchmyvaginadentatabarrelingdownthehighway

MOORHEN OF DHARMA

Like that icon I can weep from my sternum

        And on particularly tragic days
        From the left thumb

PELICAN OF HOKEY POKEY

    all tree frogs hiding, afflicted,

    in calabashes make

    your offerings now

    the ancestors are coming

SHRIKE OF PEPTIDES

    The largest animals
                are also the gentlest
    Yet headlines read,   *Hulking*
                Arctic Monsters
        Run
                    Amok!

and agate glaciers
                    torn asunder
Find it here, in me, then—
                the largesmall
made benign—
            newborn grass
                            piercing
            the black
and moldering
                stacks
                    of hay bales
                on my cliffs
                    cantering
within
        are ten thousand
                        wild
horses—
                    But only I=
                        Can drink=
                    Their milk

                    from *Verse*

The Old Woman Gets Drunk with the Moon

◇   ◇   ◇

The moon is rising everywhere—
The moon's my favorite rocking chair,
My tin pot-top, my green plum tree,
My brassy buttoned cavalry
Tap-dancing up a crystal stair.

O watch them pitch and take the air!
Like shoo fly pies and signal flares,
Like clotted cream and bumblebees,
The moons are rising.

How hits-the-spot, how debonair,
What swooned balloons of savoir faire,
What purr of rain-blurred bright marquees
That linger late, that wait for me,
Who'll someday rest my cold bones there
In moons that rise up everywhere.

from *Pleiades*

DOLLY LEMKE

I never went to
that movie at 12:45

◊   ◊   ◊

I wasn't honest with most of my boyfriends.
I just wanted to have as much sex as possible.
I never told my mom the real reason I got my tongue pierced.
The cigarettes that weren't mine were actually mine, every time.

I'm not really okay with being alone in any sense.
I have been afraid of the dark since I was 6 years old.
I wish girls liked me more.
There is an exact ratio of coffee, cream, and sugar in every cup I drink.
Half the books I own I have never read.

I am nervous for my blood work to come back.
The countless times I have called my gynecologist in panic.
The countless times I have had to ask for help because I don't have insurance.
He asked me when I was getting married.
The scale must be wrong.

I got so excited about a sealing wax set and an orange serving spoon at an estate
        sale.
The feeling I got about buying something from an estate sale.
I love crafts made by elderly women: pressed flower cards, doilies, and knit
        pot-holders.
I will go deeply in debt for vintage dresses that sway lightly in my closet.
I spent $192 at the Antique Mart on Broadway today: a 1960's Mod Print dress,
        a 1950's solid wood bedside table, a sequins party dress.

The number of times I have to inventory our relationship before you forget
      where I am.
I purposefully call you when you are sleeping, so "we must have just missed
      each other."
How much I would rather not do this.
How much I love doing this.

from *Columbia Poetry Review*

A Man with a Rooster in His Dream

◇　◇　◇

Alright, I'll tell you the weirdo dream
I had, but before I unwind that yarn,

let's twist our common thread. Like you,
I stare plumb through the wall sometimes,

because I'm thinking of a tree
and a little tenant house beside it,

and you-know-who on the stone step watching
as I pretend I'm a butterfly

and beg the flowers pretty please
to open wider for the bees.

That old communion scene won't go
to sleep, and I hope we both agree

it shouldn't.—Now, about that dream.
I was just a tadpole, eight or nine,

so yonder down the road from home
that when a storm had pinched the sky

into a fist and looked to shake it,
I was afraid I might get drowned or struck,

so I ran up on this widow's porch
and in the flash I saw her. She held

a hatchet in one hand and spanked its head
against her other palm. Thar, thar,

she said, hit's just a little thunder,
and cocked her head. In the corner I saw

the comb of a one-legged rooster,
bristled and bobbing up and down.

Sometime he turn so troublesome
and mean I chop his little laig off

to set him straight, but then that laig
grows back, so I chop it off again!

She cackled and pulled the porch-light string,
and pointed with the hatchet handle

to a bucket full of rooster feet,
their spurs still sharp, but clumped together

like rusty nails, and beyond the bucket
I caught the red-eyed glare of the rooster,

who hopped in place a couple of times
as if to punctuate his position.

Hit's like the devil with that rooster,
the widow woman said, around

and around—good gracious—and even when
he's down to just one bony laig

he don't set still!—You wouldn't want
a peg-leg rooster would you, boy?

That was the last the widow said.
Did I run home? Did a fist of rain

beat down on me that night; did I tuck
that rooster underneath my arm?

I could have given him a name,
or watched his little leg grow back,

poor thing, or looked him in his eye
to see if something really real

was hiding in the bloodshot room
behind it. Now, does he belong

in that communion scene with the bees
and butterflies, that honeyed day

in spring that never has a midnight?
I'm afraid he does. In fact, I think

that pretty bird is always perched
in the blown-down shadow of the tree

I make each magic night when I see
the face of love in her doorway lit

by the moon, and she draws me in. And then
I see she's staring not quite at me

but at some whimsy in the grass.
She loves that rooster more than me—

well, that's what I think, when she clenches her teeth
because that gritty word is tied

like a clover button to her tongue
and she can't decide if she should spit

or bite it into smaller words.
That's the gaze we always face,

in dreams and otherwise—the slate
of mischief mocking, mocking hope,

the imperfections of the tree,
the privations of the tenant house—

who dreamed this country hoedown up?—
the one-armed clock God's handyman

has nailed to the wall of the endless day
and wound up with a key, a key!

from *Ploughshares*

Seven Days of Falling

◊　◊　◊

Today, I'm assimilating like margarine
into hotcakes. I'm getting down

like Danny LaRusso after the against-
the-rules leg sweep. So low,

I'll be a flower in common decency's
lapel. Factual, the same way "Zanzibar"

means *sea of blacks* to anyone who isn't
from there. Where is Juan Valdez,

his burroesque dependability when
you need him? I had a friend who minted

T-shirts with Juan front and center,
an afro instead of a sombrero, a power

fist in place of a smile. The inscription:
100% Colombian. I'm going the way

of skin—radio waves, thoughts
like ear-to-ear transmissions grounded

into the ozone on the way from mindless
space to forgetful Earth. Man, my skin

doesn't need me any more than mold
needs cheese. On this day of cellophane

lunchboxes and hand grenades reshaping
my palms into their own militaristic orbit,

there are only oceans to catch me.
On this day, something needs

to catalogue me: a hall monitor
doubled wide by ambition,

a goldfish with thumbs hitchhiking
toward a fishbowl full of dub.

from *Prairie Schooner*

Pietà

◇   ◇   ◇

And *yes* the body and   the body most / Without   *yes*   *yes*

her legs and if   / She stood you said   *monstrous*

and *yes*   / And if

she stood her body standing least   / The Lord

to love the body first   destroys the body

And if she stood her body standing least

her body / *Yes*   and *yes*   *monstrous* and her   face a child's / Face

and her son's   body a child's

Body the Lord   to love the body first

Gave her a son who could not love her   *yes*

Monstrous the Lord

to love the body   punishes the body / *Yes*   with the body

The Lord   with the body and   *monstrous* with love   / And *yes* the body most   refusing *yes*   to stand

resists

from *West Branch*

JEFFREY McDANIEL

The Grudge

◊ ◊ ◊

I watered the grudge,
not with the fervent devotion
of a nun clutching rosary beads,
not with the destructive clockwork
of a drunk spilling vodka
tumblers on the cactus erupting
through his heart, but I watered it,
went out there at midnight,
with a can of spittle, moon dangling
like a lightbulb from its frail cord,
and I dripped the dark
nourishing fluid into its roots,
my face pulsing like a blister
as the venom petals bloomed.

from *Sonora Review*

Identity

◊   ◊   ◊

When Hans Hofmann became a hedgehog
somewhere in a Germany that has
vanished with its forests and hedgerows
Shakespeare would have been a young actor
starting out in a country that was
only a word to Hans who had learned
from those who had painted animals
only from hearing tales about them
without ever setting eyes on them
or from corpses with the lingering
light mute and deathly still forever
held fast in the fur or the feathers
hanging or lying on a table
and he had learned from others who had
arranged the corpses of animals
as though they were still alive in full
flight or on their way but this hedgehog
was there in the same life as his own
looking around at him with his brush
of camel hair and his stretched parchment
of sheepskin as he turned to each sharp
particular quill and every black
whisker on the long live snout and those
flat clawed feet made only for trundling
and for feeling along the dark undersides
of stones and as Hans took them in he
turned into the Hans that we would see

from *Poetry*

Letter to the Past
after Long Silence

◇   ◇   ◇

Don't be alarmed. I come unarmed,
or, at least, undrawn. No claws, no

bombs, no mobs, I promise. Odd,
how I've forgotten, this soft fog

clotting my brain. Gone, the long
reign of hate, the tight rein of terror,

gone, the arid air laced with mace.
I'd wager you wish to live in peace,

to wake at night to silence, no guns,
no thunder, flame and plunder, just

a cadence of rain, each drop erasing
failure's stale taste. And I'd bet

my name dismays you greatly, so
let me state my case. To be plain,

I miss you, I know it sounds inane.
Your stagey ways, your feinting,

the shameless parlor games. Tell me,
are shards still shaken into your eyes,

your hair as dark as starlings? Are you
still arch, charming, artful, on guard?

Ardent, jarring, sparring with the stars?
Tell me, how does your garden grow?

You know, it wasn't all hell, swelter,
swelling, trembling, the shells pelting

our tents. Welts, welter, wreckage,
the stench of fly-specked flesh. Hell,

some nights the sky held only bells,
the dells welled with light, my head

bent to the fire where you knelt, deftly
dealt the deck, fortune-telling, sending

velvet spells. Do I digress? I guess
I meant to say a blessing, pay a debt,

but my tongue is heavy as felt. Listen,
I am climbing memory's slippery rungs.

Listen, my hands are cold. Oh, I know
it is over, stilled. Still, you filled my lungs

with summer. The town was one tunnel
of green. And I was still a girl, twirling

in the trees, my body softened by August,
my heart humming, a field full of bees.

Love, it is a little lonely without you.
I sit on the porch swing and whistle,

but stillness still stings. Love, I loved
your stories. Above all other things.

from *New England Review*

EILEEN MYLES

The Perfect Faceless Fish

◊ ◊ ◊

It is a miracle
that I should speak
to delight you.
I feel like a flag
more or less
but music is my breeze
I have many friends
rest assured.
You have given me
my water
and for this I must
thank you. You have
been described
as elegant in your time
and it is long
the road to go
I am honored to accompany
you. A picture
is simply what I am
an old crease
a perfect book
you will miss me
in your sterile anticipation
of something to hang
this picture on. I come
& go. An edible saint.
But if you feast
on me you will be hungry.

I know your intelligence
carnal somehow
and I began to speak
when you began to want
me. Please don't interrupt
I cross my legs
I flood the darkened
rooms of art

for a while.
And frankly that moment
is gone.
We could only talk through
our eyes and now
that is gone. But this
is deeper than
the marrow
we don't need rods cones
those sanskrit piles of things
I am seeing through a stain
right now
in your love
I am swimming for years.
In a sudden absence
of trouble in a deftly
handled conversation
I, a luminous fish
felt in this spectacle of impossibility
a fragrant graze upon the
world
an intermittent twitch,
whisper. If I had hands
I would touch everyone
I vanish in the green
of the background
that goes on and on
made by those who recognize
it that way
there is always something better

to do
I live in a terminal
and so do you
listen we are trying to end everything
by this enormous silence
brief
but it was the old thing
so it shall be very loud
very loutish in the squabbles we
have about right & wrong
& where the flagpole is and
do we ever
will we ever have enough
space to play the game
I am deeply knowing you
and feel you have chosen
me for this conversation
before it's cooked
before anything is prepared
anything at all
the lesser details never mind
the first exquisite choice
that brought me into being
this conversation
a fishy birth
I've had you in my pocket
it's all that I know
but a knowing that is useless
without this acknowledgment
in a many chambered room
ew
is that what you said
enormous darkly I accept it
I flow around and fold
into everything your comic
desultory contempt
which I'm beginning to see
functions as glue
for you

the prettiness for me is
the opening city
and moving through it with you
the young old fold
around your mouth
seismic
trust that
I am gold in the reconciliation
gold in the anticipation
paradise great ambiance
what's available
is not of any use to
what is me today
a stoic longing symbol of
studying peace
in outlandish quarters
your long room in the night
your whole long body
which is faceless too
to acquire your trust is of
utmost importance to me
I am foolish I talking fish
the time is here for me
to make promises to
you that is sometimes standing
in a bakery
laughing becomes a professional
wife with empty folders
and I see the muscle
embedded the one
that can't be removed
in the beloved text that is
offered
a torso sized drink to me
each time I break the surface
turn around
bubbles cascading from
the incommensurate
path of my tale, tentacle

limbs
you make me enough
so I hold a cup
gasping with laughter
in the T-shirts covered with
arcane scribbles
carry the message
awkward grins and phones to
their ears
yours are wired to everything
there is
you're an impossible telephone
I lift my head for the
last sip of your
ew
a lamb leaps over the fins
the arms I would
have we would hold
each other in
I am waiting. No difficulty
with gold. As I told
your mother I have
obtained access
to an uncontrolled intimacy
fear not
certainly I did not phrase it
that like
but I met her in
the most advanced
communication terrain
and exchanged
messages concerning our
difficulties with god
and man
I am beginning to know
I am gold a transforming
ship
the clipped end of an
utterance I was saving
for you when I saw your

swinging light
the door approach
and everything moves
    close

from *The Brooklyn Rail*

CAMILLE NORTON

The Prison Diary
of Bartlett Yancey Malone

◇   ◇   ◇

Point Lookout Penitentiary for Confederate Soldiers, Maryland 1864

Mister Morgan of South Carolina is my teacher.
He took the cook house for our school.
I write these words in a book he gave me:

Consort is a husband or wife.
Concert is a harmony.
Disease is sickness. Decease means death.
Foul is filthy and fowl is a bird
such as those we have at hand in the camp
but can never grasp: wild swans,
big by half as a man's body,
gulls that are wilder still.
Peahens we have none.
Quail seek higher ground
than what we lie on.

This is a strange ambiguity.

We are 16 men to a tent,
three men to a blanket.
They say we number 18,000.

The 6th was cold and cloudy and we had nine men to die at Hospital.
The 7th was very cool and a small snow fell.
The 10th was nice and I saw the man who makes the coffins.

The 22nd of January 64 was a very pritty day and it was my birthday,
which maid me 25 years of age.
I feasted on crackers and coffee.

Toward evening the air changed and the night was very cold.
Five of our men froze to death before morning.
Two was so hungry they caught a Rat
and cooked him and ate him.

Last night. I dreamed of Mrs. Greenhow's escape
from the Old Capitol Prison.
She was flying far above the Chesapeake.
When I reached out to touch her
she wrapt me in her skirt.

I have not got any shoes.

I was borned in the Year of our Lord 1838.
Raised and graduated in the Corn field & Tobacco patch.
The first day of July 1861 I left home.

Earthborn is to spring from the earth.
Earthbound to be confined by it.
Erenow I was nobody.
Erelong I will be nobody still.

I would tell you my poem of the breach,
how we escape like a sip through straw.

Whether you believe it or not,
whether or not you believe,

we slip through.

from *FIELD*

From Eurynome's Sandals

◇   ◇   ◇

I'm a spirit that has come a long way. Try to destroy me,
you'll find I'm permanent. I'll live on, though the people fade,
migrating across desecrated countries with dying climates.
Eurynome my name. Did I create the universe? It emerged
from my head and my feet. I'm not gonna die.

    Time, the man, chose death. But the women, too, stole my jewels,
my created beauties; they mocked them the way men mock women.
Dragged my necklaces of mountains and rivers across the floor of this
heaven, polluting them with their jealousy. You cannot create a world
of pure splendor; you must dabble in vaginal fluids forming a mucus-
and-spit-type image of yourself like us. They ripped the surfaces from
my creation. The ocean turned acid, and the sun burned us up. The
men, the women, who cares who did it? They all did.

    In all creation myths, there is something already there, it is I, danc-
ing and flirting with a scaly other. Even chaos is I. I love your terrors of
darkness and who sees it, sex the illusion of two.

The deity who arose from my mind was a dancer.
That is, moved to a rhythm with prehensile feet—poet—
big brown toes, a few hairs there. You're dancing on me
said the cosmic dragon, the galactic surface of all we can see.
So fucking what? she said. He wrapped himself around her
intensifying, then killing, her freedom—a new rhythm.
I am the goddess of all things. I am about to give birth
to beauty, migrants, savage light of every kind.
The light is bloodthirsty and will smash your collarbone
with a spear or a bomblet. I am the dance and its decline,

dear November day of stinking cars. And the same colors
yellow, orange, my feet stamped out on your surface
pressed from the first metallic tubes. Amber, vermillion, kissy
opposites. Goose-turd green.

Everything sprang up right away, by my lights, forwards and back-
wards: earth time, a human invention, is slower than bacterial time and
faster than my own time, which only does beats. I am, like, timeless.

The serpentine filmmaker, either my nemesis or lover,
can be too earnest. We're dying, he says, I intend to direct
a final masterpiece. I want to film thankless chaos
if that's what we're moving towards—or is it death? It
must be a quality within us. I'm bored, I say.
If you cared you'd star in my film. Leave me alone. The world's
ending! Well, I'm thinking . . . brooding over the first misty damp.
I was there, weren't you? It's just like always, he says
I can't rely on you, after millions of years. Wrap myself around you
so you won't get away. But as you know I'm not just here, I say, I'm
everywhere. I'm staying with him in the cheap hotel of the world.

I had many pairs of shoes at that time but principally some black
leather T-straps with flat soles; also a type of medium heel, but these
were decorated with sequined florettes, pale chartreuse outer-leaf
design and scarlet petals. I took them off one night after dancing; from
the darkness of the shoes sprang Jealousy, Fear, Cowardice, Betrayal,
Pretention, Cruelty, Violence. I watched them fly up with dispassion,
for I am unethical. They had black gauzy wings and small sarcastic
faces; little bitches and ambitious pricks. How can we change in order
to continue as our flaws scour the globe, our habitation made desert and
unpotable floodwaters? I will keep creating.

The filmmaker expresses his love for me in his face, his
litup skin, for he is also an actor. Through his huge glasses
the significance in his green eyes must conquer.
I am loving him back, by looking a certain way too.
He has to leave me to work on his movie, which will fascinate me
and which I'll loathe; he is fashioning the species agreement that
surfaces be nonchaotic—even when he insists he's filming disorder.

His is not the world I created, for it is in time and doomed to end.
Well that's just his planet. I tell you creation is not so automatized.

The people go everywhere, in the first days, out of curiosity; though
now we are frantic, they say. For example the desertification of Africa
pushes us towards the garbage-clogged Mediterranean. We are called
illegal immigrants and turned back, but we are the people, on the move
as ever. I am the man you are, not a genetic other—Give me succour and
I'll strengthen your land with my muscles and songs; individual unhap-
piness/happiness makes anyone act like a jerk, hating the sight of me. I am
not your emotional burden: it comes from your own imperfect abilities.

I am unethical and immoral, or I wouldn't have made anything:
it does what it wants, after all. Then they dislike me for that,
they say I'm not philosophical enough—philosophical?
The little technocratic sillies can't figure out where life comes from.
It's too fast for splitting hairs, babe; you design an engine and
presto cars and planes surround you like cholera germs.
I can do Life—as in entering it: but I pull out before long.
Did I create the dragonsnake film guy? I hardly know.
Sometimes I am almost in thrall to him, but then
I realize it's time to leave, tiptoe out through the back door.
Go off to a planet whose creatures aren't so damned mean.

One of the most beautiful things was the tattered smell of emeralds.
Also, the calculation in spittle that made it malleable and endless, shapes
of an Orion or Ophiacus. The undifferentiated visionary organ navigates
possibility all the time. But I can be finite like a human, sudden in the
real. *Real,* like the delusion of credit: you get *credit* for what you do? You
have an exquisitely individual clitoris. The storm is scorched by some-
one's intelligence, but whose? Why, mine! Who am in all times at once.

My breasts are covered with blood, you can film that, I say.
Or is it light, infrared, of some dead star over there?
Chaos, I continue, could be quieter than everyone thinks,
almost sullen . . . You really have blood on your breasts! No, it's
just red light, he says. The creation is intense, I remind him,
when I'm in it I reflect red. Well I'm always in it. But sometimes
I wear its color just for you. Blood's of such interest to you, them—

they did a lot of killing to become themselves, the people, not that they
had to. They'd kill someone to see if he died, because they weren't sure.
I'd left it at that because I wasn't sure: they're pumped full of blood,
will they leave it inside, or will they always try to see it? You're so perverse,
he says. Oh, everyone's a critic! Leave the opus alone and no one dies.
They just have to poke a needle in an eyeball, don't they?

The people always reconfigure in the kaleidoscope of their history and
hail their new direction. One is truly past caring; their penchant for organi-
zation is always their undoing. I never even suggested that they have foun-
dation myths, governments, justice; I've never told them anything. I make
things—I thought they might like it, a world. It's not such a big deal, it isn't
really all that you know, if you stop and think about it. Everything you can
think of, there's that too.

So one of us touches the other's face: the camera's on us, he says.
You want us to look like two actors, I say: Why?
You can't just be yourself in a room full of light, he says,
All the human migratory routes are in this chamber, map
beneath the skin; I can remember when I crossed the wide Missouri—
though there's more than one Missouri. Why focus so hard? I say.
I want to cross one Missouri, make love to one body—Kisses my navel.
The camera is supposed to be like the sky, but I am the sky. If
I break his camera, this moment won't happen . . . I despise it, he
invented it. I'm not ethical enough to break it: I tend to let creation
do what it wants. I grab my clothes, throw them on—Don't—dammit—
don't mess everything up! Shit, you're such a little prima donna.

The people walk everywhere observing. Birds are more talented than I
am, more beautiful. If I'm like a monkey, still I can't swing from tree to tree.
I can't disappear like a snake, can't live underwater, can't make honey, can't
tear you to pieces with my claws.

The people at first long to be as great as the other creatures, then they
begin to destroy them out of some narcissism or disinterest. They lose sym-
pathy with whatever they didn't make themselves.

The people have words; they use them to pretend with. *There is no such
thing as pretending, it's all real! No nothing's real*—you can say shit like that.
You can say anything; you can believe anything, to the depths of your soul,
or not.

The people have lost their first concentration; they do what they do, dumb fucks.

How did you get here? That's just a question. There isn't any reason why you shouldn't always have been, despite appearances, the seeming births and deaths. Are you really bound by the finite body you name? The people realized they were the birds and snakes— before they forgot—they knew what it felt like to fly and to slither without arms; they knew what it felt like to be the ground holding them up. Brother dirt and sister rock; mother the vault of sky, father lightning. This is sentimental or conventional— oh I'm so glad you know, you jealous bitch. We migrated from Asia to Australia, because we wanted to see what was happening. A lot's going on, but it appears to be dying in the future.

I remember Harry the gigolo—they said he was a gigolo. Belonged to a fraternity. He was a couple years older than I. So a group of us went way uptown to someone's apartment—a party, and he—we'd never spoken— beckoned me into an empty bedroom. We made love quietly and then rejoined the others; I never saw him again. He was a sweet lover, and this is a happy moment in the mind of god.

What I seemed to have was a lot of stuff. I liked my stuff, which had always been around—quasi-material shapes, colors, mementos from the past or future. So he'd already organized some of time's surfaces— snaky mosaics curving—time is whose mind bending, bending, you big stupid snake. So he's always shooting footage, chopping off two-hour lengths, and I'm always messing things up, having more thoughts injecting inconsistency into the unretractable glittering fabric with its ataxic panoramas of violence: intergalactic storms, or some minor species events, the wars of their tininess. A lot of worlds brought forth at the feet of the creator. The human story is sort of like all the others. Are all art works interchangeable? This is a rubellite, a kind of tourmaline, red, with hexagonal long prismatic crystals. And here's a most beautiful form, the face of a worn boulder

beige with a trace of rust color, you can find these on many
planets. Not exactly a species. I'm peaceful with them.

I am dying of hunger, for . . . everything I've made. I am making it;
then it's made; then, the future of its destruction. Again I say, I thought
you would like it, but—was I so hungry? What if I just sat still?

They often feel the world is a grotesque enigma, that they are that;
the people, the billions of souls. At first they marveled, but then they
discovered they were dying of hunger for . . .

I am as hungry to be lonely as I am for the sound of the filmmaker's
steps on the floor. But I'm most hungry to have made all there is, for
you.

Then I withdraw; I'm bored. The people, for example, are so bor-
ing. They kill each other obsessively in wars; who they used to be goes
absent; they can only do this killing now, believing they have lost their
souls, so the imagined hell-figure smiles at them, real with his gaunt
face, blood in its creases. You believe in me, he says. I'm here when you
need me.

At dawn a rose-peach cloud, dissolving into cerulean over
bare twigs, several yellow leaves; magpies. I'm amazed.
The filmmaker has taken pains to bleach out the rose and blue; it
shouldn't be so blatant if the climate is dying. But I require
mysticism here, he says, I'll place the cloud behind the head
of an avenger: There has to be an Avenging Angel. I
object, I say. It's such a flat, dumb thing, this avenging the people do.
We have to have a lot of shootouts, he says, against a scary
chemical sky: they symbolize the wars themselves, which are too
chaotic to show meaning. I want disgust, futility, hope.
There's not enough depth, oh your art's too finite.
You only give them flatness—a screen—I guess it's as flat
as most ideas; but we've got a myriadly dimensioned universe.
They chose their flat eyes, he says, chose them! Sort of, I
say. He says, I intend plenty of desolation, pylons in flames;
dams crumble. Engineers are the real artists, aren't they?—
all their works eroded or abandoned. I keep being here, I say,
in this screening room moment: I've been in this moment for
fucking ever: time to sit back and watch the Magellanic Clouds

move, just move. All of that will end too, he says. I'm
the one who would know! I snap. Oh, don't you just know everything!
But no one cares about knowing. They like moving snapshots
of grim-faced heroes, coping. Killing. A portrait of knowing, yes, but
not Knowing itself. No one can stand it, except for you.

from *Chicago Review*

Q

◇   ◇   ◇

Q belonged to Q.&A.,
to questions, and to foursomes, and fractions,
it belonged to the Queen, to Quakers, to quintets—
within its compound in the dictionary dwelt
the quill pig, and quince beetle,
and quetzal, and quail. Quailing was part of Q's
quiddity—the Q quaked
and quivered, it quarrelled and quashed. No one was
quite sure where it had come from, but it had
travelled with the K, they were the two voiceless
velar Semitic consonants, they went
back to the desert, to *caph* and *koph*.
And K has done a lot better—
29 pages in Webster's Third
to Q's 13. And though Q has much
to be proud of, from Q.&I. detector
through quinoa, sometimes these days the letter
looks like what medical students called the
Q face—its tongue lolling out.
And sometimes when you pass a folded
newspaper you can hear from within it
a keening, from all the Q's who are being
set in type, warboarded,
made to tell and tell of the quick and the
Iraq dead.

from *The New Yorker*

GREGORY PARDLO

Written by Himself

◊ ◊ ◊

I was born in minutes in a roadside kitchen a skillet
whispering my name. I was born to rainwater and lye;
I was born across the river where I
was borrowed with clothespins, a harrow tooth,
broadsides sewn in my shoes. I returned, though
it please you, through no fault of my own,
pockets filled with coffee grounds and eggshells.
I was born still and superstitious; I bore an unexpected burden.
I gave birth, I gave blessing, I gave rise to suspicion.
I was born abandoned outdoors in the heat-shaped air,
air drifting like spirits and old windows.
I was born a fraction and a cipher and a ledger entry;
I was an index of first lines when I was born.
I was born waist-deep stubborn in the water crying
                ain't I a woman and a brother I was born
to this hall of mirrors, this horror movie I was
born with a prologue of references, pursued
by mosquitoes and thieves, I was born passing
off the problem of the twentieth century: I was born.
I read minds before I could read fishes and loaves;
I walked a piece of the way alone before I was born.

from *American Poetry Review*

LUCIA PERILLO

Inseminating the Elephant

◇   ◇   ◇

The zoologists who came from Germany
wore bicycle helmets and protective rubber suits.
So as not to be soiled by substances
that alchemize to produce laughter in the human species;
how does that work biochemically is a question
whose answer I have not found yet. But these are men
whose language requires difficult conjugations under any circumstance:
first, there's the matter of the enema, which ought to come
as no surprise. Because what the news brings us
is often wheelbarrows of dung—suffering,
with photographs. And so long as there is suffering,
there should be also baby elephants—especially this messy,
headlamp-lit calling-forth. The problem lies
in deciding which side to side with: it is natural
to choose the giant rectal thermometer
over the twisted human form,
but is there something cowardly in that comic swerve?
Hurry an elephant
to carry the bundle of my pains,
another with shiny clamps and calipers
and the anodyne of laughter. So there, now I've alluded
to my body that grows ever more inert—better not overdo
lest you get scared; the sorrowing world
is way too big. How the zoologists start
is by facing the mirror of her flanks,
that foreboding luscious place where the gray hide
gives way to a zeroing-in of skin as vulnerable as an orchid.
Which is the place to enter, provided you are brave,
brave enough to insert your laser-guided camera

to avoid the two false openings of her "vestibule,"
much like the way of entering death, of giving birth to death,
calling it forth as described in the Tibetan Book.
And are you brave enough to side with laughter
if I face my purplish, raw reflection
and attempt the difficult entry of that chamber where
the seed-pearl of my farce and equally opalescent sorrow
lie waiting?

                    from *Poets & Writers*

Heaven and Earth

◇   ◇   ◇

For days now, vertigo. Conqueror-birds. Place where
suffering and a gift for it for a moment meet,
then go their separate ways. *I keep meaning to stop,*
to wait for you. Places where, all but untrackably, fear—
which is animal, and wild, and almost always
worth trusting—becomes cowardice: fear given
consciousness of a finite existence in the realm
of time—what exists,

                      and doesn't. Last night,
a stillness like that of moss; like permission when it's
not been given, yet not withheld exactly. Across the dark—
through it—the occasional handful of notes: someone
else out there, singing? or myself singing,
and the echoing after? I didn't know,

                          or want to. A map
unfolding, getting folded back up again, seeming
sometimes—even as I held it—to be on fire:
It had seemed my life. What am I, that I should stand
so apart from my own happiness? The stars did
what they do, mostly: looked unbudging, transfixed,
like cattle asleep in a black pasture, all the restlessness
torn out of them, away, done with. I turn beneath them.

from *Witness*

Domain

◇　◇　◇

1

A girl looks through a microscope her father's
showing her life
in a drop of water or
finger blood smeared onto a glass wafer

Later leaning head on hand
while the sound of scales being practiced
clambers bleakly, adamantly up the stairs
she reads her own handwriting

Neighbors don't meet on the corner here
the child whose parents aren't home is not offered a meal
the congressman's wife who wears nothing but green
tramples through unraked oakleaves yelling
                    to her strayed dogs *Hey Rex! Hey Roy!*
husband in Washington: 1944

The girl finding her method: you want friends,
you're going to have to write
letters to strangers

A coffee-stain splashed on a desk: her accident her
mistake her true
country: wavy brown coastline upland
silky reeds swayed by long lectures of the wind

From the shore small boats reach, depart, return
the never-leavers tie nets of dried seaweed weighted
with tumbled-down stones
instruct young fingers through difficult knots
guiding, scraping some young fingers
No sound carries far from here

Rebuked, utopian projection

she visits rarely trying to keep
the interior root-systems, milky
nipples of stars, airborne wings rushing over

refuge of missing parts

intact

from *Michigan Quarterly Review*

JAMES RICHARDSON

Vectors 2.3: Fifty Aphorisms and Ten-Second Essays

◇   ◇   ◇

1. The odds against today were insurmountable, until it happened.
2. Thoughts are discussed, opinions displayed.
3. Clarity's not light. It's the angle that suddenly lets you see through the window's glare, the pond's reflections.
4. Spontaneity takes a few rehearsals.
5. There are two kinds of people in the world . . . and who is not both of them?
6. Work is required play.
7. Slug, fungus: part of your body has fallen out. Snake, rat: part of it might try to get back in.
8. Loving yourself is about as likely as tickling yourself.
9. To be Cool is to play at being Cold. Hot, too, is play, and more like Cool than Warm: no one exclaims delightedly "Man, that's *Warm!*" We'll pay to watch the act of Hot and Cool, but we flee the salesmen, priests and presidents playing Warm.
10. No one's so entertaining as the one who thinks you are.
11. Everyone's psyched that elections are decided by a single vote! That it's a close game! That choice approximates chance!
12. Build bottom up, clean top down.
13. Office supplies stores are the Cathedrals of Work in General. They forgive, they console, they promise a new start. These supplies have done work like yours a million times. Maybe when you get home it will already be finished.
14. When it gets ahead of itself, the wave breaks.
15. I'd listen to my conscience if I could be sure it was really mine.
16. The way our walk changes entering a store or museum, slowing,

widening a little, eyes sweeping level. Foraging on the ancient savanna for something to eat, something to use.

17. The lesser of two evils is the one with the less evil friends.

18. The boutique wants you to think you're a collector, the discounter that you're a burglar.

19. Only your unnoticed victories last: the rest are avenged.

20. He's angry at the wronged for making the world unjust.

21. Listen hardest to the one you hope is not telling the truth.

22. Nothing dirtier than old soap.

23. How comforting your paranoia: someone's listening, someone's watching, someone's thinking about you all the time.

24. Snakes cannot back up.

25. The speckled wall-to-wall, the patterned shirt *don't show dirt*. Sometimes, truth be damned, we need to be relieved from seeing. As with allergies, the response is a bigger problem than the problem.

26. What keeps us deceived is the hope that we aren't.

27. Nothing important comes with instructions.

28. Don't trust the revolutionist with your freedom: he's an authoritarian who happens to be out of power.

29. I've lived here so long I trip on what has been gone for years.

30. Knowing how to be pleased with what's there is a great secret of happy living, sensitive reading, and bad writing.

31. The ascetic's last pleasure is blaming you for all he has forgone.

32. How badly I'd like to believe that my cherished reasonableness and heavily defended calm could rule the world. But as things are, somebody has to feel too much, somebody has to speak too loud, somebody has to be completely unreasonable.

33. For Sisyphus the trouble of pushing the rock uphill was worth it for the thrill of watching it smash all before it on the way down.

34. Do unto others and an eye for an eye have the same payment plan.

35. The modesty of avoiding repetition involves the vanity of thinking everyone must have been listening the first time.

36. I'm a little scared of the ocean, thinking it might at any minute throw itself over me and the tiny continents. So much harder to see what's holding *others* back.

37. Our resolutions for self-control are like our wars for peace.

38. The great man's not sure he wants you to criticize even his great rival, lest there be no such thing as greatness.

39. The will has a will of its own.

40. My best critic is me, too late.

41. It's not success but self-congratulation that the Furies scent.

42. When you think in words, are you sure it's your own voice you hear?

43. At first skepticism keeps you from being too much like everyone else, then, you hope, from being too much like yourself.

44. If you think you might be lost, you are. If you know you're lost, you're at least free to look for the way.

45. Of course I'm an escapist. I'm trying to get somewhere real.

46. You find your marginalia in a book and realize that for decades you have been walking in circles.

47. As for my writing. I like it enough to keep going. I dislike it enough to keep going.

48. A knot is strings getting in each other's way. What keeps us together is what keeps us apart.

49. That one thing in life I'm meant to do?—well, I have to finish this first.

50. Closing a door very gently, you pull with one hand, push with the other.

from *American Poetry Review*

Children's Children Speech

◇   ◇   ◇

What would we want our luckless heirs to say,
Now that we too globally see it will end—
The bees, the buds, the mercurial sea, the air
All spoiled—that we made waste of miracles?

Now that we're so globally sure it will end,
We should prepare a speech defending all
The spoils we've made so much of. Miracles
Are merely things we think we don't deserve.

We may as well prepare it now, the speech
That would explain the things we had to have
Were merely things we thought we would deserve
In a heaven we had stopped believing in.

That would explain *some* things. We had to have
Whatever made us feel above the land,
So that the heaven we'd stopped believing in
Could be had *here,* by plane or satellite.

We craved what made us feel above the land
Whose laws were fixed to leave us in the dirt.
What could be seen by plane or satellite
Was fast depleting: ice floe, forest, meadow—

Whose dirty laws were fixed, made by that god
Who'd also made our minds that made whatever
Fast depleted ice floe, forest, meadow.
Any speech we have a mind to write

Our mind's made up to stand behind, whatever
We may do to bees, or seas, or air
Empowering speech. We have a mind to write
Our luckless heirs, but what's the use? They'll call us

They. "*They* did this. We weren't even there."

from *The Georgia Review*

Having My Say-So

◇　◇　◇

What a sweet dear good boy he is, I said aloud to the empty room.
I never expected to feel like Elizabeth Barrett Browning again, not this soon.
It's not so soon.
Surely it's undignified for a gent to want to take another gent bouquets, and
　　　　absurd?
Just as surely I could not care less.
Surely it's an incredible invasion of someone else's privacy to sit around writing
　　　　unsolicited poems to and about him?
Well, as you-know-who would say,
I'm sorry but I just can't help it I feel this way.
Deeply.
What kind of thing does a man say to a man he's in love with?
Things like, I can't tell you how adorable you looked in your new suit and that
　　　　tie the other night.
Then he says, That suit is rather me isn't it,
then I say, Yes,
and the world lights up like the hot star they say it used to be
or may become,
burnt by the sun.
It's still glowing!
That's not my sleeve, that's my heart.
Not less than any other lover who ever wrote I want to describe
his looks, the way his wide eyebrows uniquely die away in a haze of fine short
　　　　hairs on the east and west slopes of his forehead,
the way they join in a tuft, a small explosion of longer hairs above his nose,
　　　　the crinkled pink of a new small scar, still touched by the black recent
　　　　stitches,
the fullness of his lower lip, like the excess that shaped the pear, sulky and
　　　　determined, boyish and sweet,

Greek, before they got refined:
but if I'm such a lover why can't I remember the color of his eyes?
I know their movements, how they twinkle wickedly (love is all about clichés)
when he's silly-drunk and cute,
how animal and slitty they get when he's tired,
their hard look at the floor when he won't be shy:
I think they're the color of the sky, which is not always blue.
Then there's his jaw that has a longbow curve to it
his hair curling on his nape, not silky or wiry, lively,
and in a quick transition to a longer view
the thin-skinned very naked whiteness of his back with muscles lapped and
        moving in it,
his belly, firm as a flank, sprouting little curves like dune grass around the Lake
        Nemi of his navel:
Moon! look down and see the small dark pit of your reflection on this pale
        shaded plain of flesh.
Heart, dream no further:
do you want to go off like the rockets on the Fourth at the Washington
        Monument?
I must get back to work,
but first I'll look at the clock and imagine where he is.

from *The Sienese Shredder*

Allison Wolff

◇　◇　◇

Like a river at night, her hair,
the sky starless, streetlights
glossing the full dark of it:
Was she Jewish? I was seventeen,

an "Afro-American" senior
transferred to a suburban school
that held just a few of us.
And she had light-brown eyes

and tight tube tops   and skin
white enough to read by
in a dim room. It was impossible
not to be curious.

Me and my boy, Terry, talked about
"pink honeys" sometimes: we watched
I Dream of Jeannie and could see Barbara
Eden—in her skimpy finery—lounging

on our very own lonely sofas.
We wondered what white girls were
really like, as if they'd been raised
by the freckled light of the moon.

I can't remember Allison's voice
but the loud tap of her strapless heels
clacking down the halls is still clear.
Autumn, 1972: Race was the elephant

sitting on everyone. Even
as a teenager, I took the weight
as part of the weather, a sort of heavy
humidity felt inside and in the streets.

One day, *once upon a time,* she laughed
with me in the cafeteria—something
about the tater tots, I guess,
or the electric-blue Jell-O. Usually,

it was just some of us displaced brothers
talkin' noise, clowning around, so she
caught all of us way off-guard. Then,
after school, I waved   and she smiled

and the sun was out—that three o'clock,
after-school sun rubbing the sidewalk
with the shadows of trees—

and while the wind pitched the last
of September, we started talking
and the dry leaves shook and sizzled.

In so many ways, I was still a child,
though I wore my seventeen years
like a matador's cape.

The monsters that murdered
Emmett Till—were they everywhere?
I didn't know. I didn't know enough

to worry enough about the story
white people kept trying to tell.
And, given the thing that America is,
maybe sometimes such stupidity works
for the good. Occasionally,

History offers a reprieve, everything
leading up to a particular moment

suddenly declared a mistrial:
so I'm a black boy suddenly

walking the Jenkintown streets
with a white girl—so ridiculously
conspicuous   we must've been
invisible. I remember her mother

not being home and cold Coca-Cola
in plastic cups and the delicious
length of Allison's tongue   and
we knew, without saying anything,
we were kissing the *color line*

goodbye and on and on for an hour
we kissed, hardly breathing, the light almost
blinding whenever we unclosed our eyes—
as if we had discovered the dreaming door
to a different country   and were walking

out   as if we *could* actually
walk the glare we'd been
born into: as if my hand
on her knee, her hand
on my hand, my hand
in her hair, her mouth
on my mouth   opened
and opened and opened

from *Ploughshares*

A Visit

◇　◇　◇

It was a small family party
Aunt Olive who tried to save Dallas
pleased after death to have a park
named after her after death
Terrified I got up off my usual position
and didn't know whether to look or think
Afraid of an encapsulated psychosis
They were quiet: Elaine and Bill de Kooning took a look
and Kenneth so happy, surprised to have a Heaven after all
I decided to accept 10,000 years of imprisonment
if that would lighten my father's obvious punishment itself
lightened by his good works for workers

Meyer Schapiro looked on steadily
as if he were watching Kings of the Road
in the scene of excretion
Nothing human or divine was strange, to him
And I had been crying when the 33 recording
of my grandfather's voice played El Mole Rachamim
And I couldn't translate
whom he was calling supplicant
I asked for something faster or fall
Then John Hejduk arrived looking for his wife son and daughter
happy as if he were building worlds again
And Fairfield in painting gear
who had predicted this before
that despite particulars something was the same

and my Uncle Bill born with an open heart
The dead were visiting
in the corridor
I was like a charlatan on TV
finding a smile (long) on the door
or like the philosopher who will always
wake and travel for a table risen
The dead were gathering, I saw them all
my calm father and my mother like two candles
And his father Aaron atheist and good chess player
who taught me to castle early and lift my violin
My father's mother whom I hardly met
walked without me with my murdered aunts
in a nest of keys and locks
They weren't singing

As others concluded I let them go—heard and listened to very little
The dead have been buried off the ground
I only saw them smile
the consolation of the need you'll say and where was Paganini,
practicing so loudly in the orchestra of heaven
where was my young dead friend Phyllis and her flute
And where I just had to look more
Before turning away in terror
A family party parting
Amateur chamber music
The delights of the dead

from *The Hat*

Carrying on like a Crow

◇   ◇   ◇

Are you authorized to speak
For these trees without leaves?
Are you able to explain
What the wind intends to do
With a man's shirt and a woman's nightgown
Left on the laundry line?
What do you know about dark clouds?
Ponds full of fallen leaves?
Old model cars rusting in a driveway?
Who gave you permission
To look at the beer can in a ditch?
The white cross by the side of the road?
The swing set in the widow's yard?
Ask yourself, if words are enough,
Or if you'd be better off
Flapping your wings from tree to tree
And carrying on like a crow?

from *London Review of Books*

Blue Yodel of Those Who Were Always Telling Me

◇   ◇   ◇

You look like you just woke up

What did you do last night
sleep in the fields

Now all of you who ride the schoolbus
during deer season be sure
and duck down on the backroads

Get on out of here

Honey Mama Julinda gone fix your eye

Sign my yearbook Don't
write anything like you did in Beth's

You know you can't come in my theatre
unless you got shoes on

Bait my hook that's what I'm paying you for

Why don't you go to Memphis
and buy your clothes

Take it from me

I ever catch you talking like that with my wife
I'll kill you you little shit

Frankie I love you really I do
with all my heart Do you
love me

Quit drinking son

You talk like a river boat gambler
You look like one

You talk like a queer
sometimes
Let me smell your fingers

Did you and one Billy Richard Willet
steal the undertaker's pick-up
break into the Junior Prom drunk
and thereby commence to dance together
like Russians on the gymnasium floor
boots and all or not

Can't you run over one measly guard
Put your heart in it

Say the five Sorrowful Mysteries
every night

O come ye sons and daughters of art

Bull

Is she stumpbroke yet

The language he loves best is the silent. . . .

Do you want me to tell her father
about you two and the Drive Inn

Had enough yet

You're no more eighteen than the man
in the moon

I just felt sorry for you
because you didn't have any folks

Over my dead body

In what year did Lord Byron write
Fare Thee Well

Go in peace

Shape up or ship out

Get off your high horse
Now get up

I say together we stand
divided we fall

You know what this means

You can bury my body down by the side
of the highway Lord my old spirit
can flag a Trailways bus and ride

from *ABZ*

GERALD STERN

Stoop

◊   ◊   ◊

While on a stoop and eating boiled beef
and while my hands are dripping with horseradish
and while a crescent moon reflects itself
in one of the windows on Sixth Avenue
near what used to be the great Balducci's
across from the woman's prison and the library,
though truth the sky is blue so it is probably
April and it's probably twenty, thirty
years ago, and I was studying women's
shoes before the long point killed the two
end toes the same time I was killing time
before the meeting at the Waverly
inside a window as I recall for I had a
burden then and I was given to meetings
like that though even then I knew what it was
like to be free of burdens for I was part
mule, wasn't I, therefore I knew what freedom
was and I am mule to this day and carry a
weight, and I will to the grave—you will see me
put it into the hole first, it is so cumbersome,
with ears the color of the sun and compromised
by wings, which I am too, and there's one mule
I knew in the late '30s whose name was Molly,
alas, not Sal, and she wasn't stupid and she was
hardly stubborn and she loved apple trees
and she was wise and loving, above rubies.

from *The Antioch Review*

SATs

◇   ◇   ◇

(1)

"Praetorian" is to the present Rome as "a classical education" is to . . .
a) willingness to pay thirty dinarii
b) a gladiator facing certain slavery
c) the abstruse shock of the new
d) the valor of examination

(2)

Your sex is to mine as a brand-new shoot is to . . .
a) pedestrian versus cyclist
b) Irenaeus versus Darwin
c) how green leaves are to old trees
d) the valor of examination

(3)

Love is to hate as the map of the world is to . . .
a) Bartolomeo Columbus in the face of Amerigo Vespucci
b) Franklin in place of Theodore, Joseph instead of Winston
c) China against America (cf *The Little Red Book*)
d) the valor of examination

We are put on this earth to pay . . .
a) God for outing us here
b) pray tell, a relinquishment of pain
c) homage to lip service in duty
d) the valor of examination

The specter of death provides . . .
a) good knees-up revelry
b) the person you always wanted
c) a devil you don't know
d) an end to examination

from *Open City*

Depression

◇   ◇   ◇

One day in summer I was walking through town looking in the store windows. I looked in the back of one and saw Wendy trying on a new dress. "You look great, Wendy," I yelled. She looked and squinted and said, "Oh, thanks Keith. I think I'll get it." I walked on. Down by the post office I ran into Mark. "Can I talk to you a second," he said. "Well, sure, Mark," I said. "Have you seen Angie?" he said. "No, I haven't," I said. "Well, she looks awful. She hasn't bathed in a week. She's depressed. She's about to lose her job. Plus, she suddenly can't stand me. I don't think she likes anybody really," he said. "Sounds like depression. My sister had it once. She also wouldn't bathe and turned on all those close to her," I said. "What did you do?" he said. "We got her to go to a doctor. He gave her some medicine and she got better," I said. "Do you remember the doctor's name?" he said. "No, but my mother might. She takes all kinds of pills. She must get them from somewhere," I said. "Well, if she'll tell you give me a call," he said. We said our goodbyes and parted. My mother had every kind of pill under the sun. She'd call me late at night and I couldn't understand her. I went on to the other stores, the gift shop, the used book store, the toy shop. I went in the toy shop. I drifted over to the table where they had all the little rubber animals. Anything you wanted for only a dollar apiece. I selected a yak, an alligator and a lamb. I paid for them up front. Then I went to the cemetery in back of the store. I found my mother's grave and placed them on it. She never did like flowers. Too much trouble.

from *Conduit*

Black Telephone

◇　◇　◇

It sits like an anvil
on end tables

in old movies
and rings—

a startling alarm—
only to advance the plot.

Or is auctioned on eBay
to aficionados of the past

who pay a fortune
to ship this relic,

this tar pit appliance
the distance it once

miraculously bridged.
Its frayed cord

a web of
dead roots.

Its dial a circle
of interminable clicks.

Its receiver a lead weight
pressing cold

dead silence
against the eavesdropping ear.

from *Tin House*

The Dark Rides

◊   ◊   ◊

The girl who likes to get high
wonders if her flower will ever unfurl,
or will there be a tight not-fully-formed
green part that chars before blooming?
Can something pinch an infant bud
so there's a missing branch forever?

Dark attractions was another
name for the dark rides:
the Gold Mine with candy wrappers
stapled to a fence for the loot,
the Black Swans "love tunnel,"
where couples whimpered
and squealed. In her underworld,
just below this one, not an inch away,
there's always a Midway strung
with garish lights, and a small paddock
of saddled ponies circling nose to tail.

To explain her own childhood, she studies
the childhood of the girl who was eventually
returned to her family unharmed,
though her bad luck dates from that time,
as well as the illusion of looking through glass.
There are lessons she's learned and unlearned
ten thousand times, caught in the drag
of one pole or another, the need to know
the wordless truth of what she is,
and the equally fierce and endless denials,

the pure-hearted questions answered by lies,
the prayers subsumed by smoke or thinned
to nothing in the fumes of alcohol.
She longs to know whatever it is
she keeps herself from knowing. Or rather,
the knowledge comes to her but she loses it
again among the small herd of centaurs
she keeps on her desk, of which only one
is female—bronze, late nineteenth-century,
grapevine crown, anatomy explicit (though tiny).
The horse's maneless neck becomes
the maiden's torso, the two bodies one.
You have to fuck the horse to fuck the girl.

from *New England Review*

Peggy Lutz, Fred Muth
12/13/08

◇ ◇ ◇

They've been in my fiction; both now dead,
Peggy just recently, long stricken (like
my Grandma) with Parkinson's disease.
But what a peppy knockout Peggy was!—
cheerleader, hockey star, May Queen, RN.
Pigtailed in kindergarten, she caught my mother's
eye, but she was too much girl for me.
Fred—so bright, so quietly wry—*his*

mother's eye fell on me, a "nicer" boy
than her son's pet pals. Fred's slight wild streak
was tamed by diabetes. At the end,
it took his toes and feet. Last time we met,
his walk rolled wildly, fetching my coat. With health
he might have soared. As was, he taught me smarts.

★

Dear friends of childhood, classmates, thank you,
scant hundred of you, for providing a
sufficiency of human types: beauty,
bully, hanger-on, natural,
twin, and fatso—all a writer needs,
all there in Shillington, its trolley cars
and little factories, cornfields and trees,
leaf fires, snowflakes, pumpkins, valentines.

To think of you brings tears less caustic
than those the thought of death brings. Perhaps
we meet our heaven at the start and not
the end of life. Even then were tears
and fear and struggle, but the town itself
draped in plain glory the passing days.

★

The town forgave me for existing; it
included me in Christmas carols, songfests
(though I sang poorly) at the Shillington,
the local movie house. My father stood,
in back, too restless to sit, but everybody
knew his name, and mine. In turn I knew
my Granddad in the overalled town crew.
I've written these before, these modest facts,

but their meaning has no bottom in my mind.
The fragments in their jiggled scope collide
to form more sacred windows. I had to move
to beautiful New England—its triple
deckers, whited churches, unplowed streets—
to learn how drear and deadly life can be.

from *The New Yorker*

149

21

◊   ◊   ◊

May my enemy be assuaged by these waves
because they are beautiful even to his evil,
may the drizzle be a benediction to his heart
even as it is to mine; they say here that the devil
is beating his wife when the sun shines through the wires
of fine, fine rain. It is not my heart that forgives
my enemy his obscene material desires
but the flare of a leaf, the dart of a mottled dove,
the processional surplices of breakers entering the cove
as penitents enter the dome to the lace of an altar;
beauty so shaping neither condemns nor saves
like the tenets of my enemy's church, the basilicas
of tumbling cherubs and agonized saints
and riots of purpureal cloud; though I have cause
I will share the world's beauty with my enemies
even though their greed destroys the innocence
of my Adamic island. My enemy is a serpent
as much as he is in a fresco, and he in all his
scales and venom and glittering head is
part of the island's beauty; he need not repent.

from *A Public Space*

G. C. WALDREP

*Their Faces
Shall Be as Flames*

◇   ◇   ◇

That was the spring the bees disappeared, we didn't know
where they went, where they'd gone, where they were going, it was a
rapture of the bees, only the weak, the young, the freshly dead
left behind, *a rapture of bees,* my neighbor with the ducks had begun to walk
like a duck, *Follow follow follow Sam* he sang as he walked, and they followed,
it was that simple, of course I thought of the Piper, although
this procession was more benign, my neighbor's I mean, though he intended
to have each for dinner, eventually, and he did not name them,
as we don't name bees, because we don't see clearly enough
to distinguish them as persons, *person* in the grammatical sense, first second
or third, which is why we refer to them in the collective, usually,
they breed, they swarm, they milk their honey for us
in the collective, and they vanish collectively, is this then the true
rapture, was the one true God after all a god of bees, and now she is taking
them home, is this any more comforting than all the other proposed
       explanations,
pesticide, fungus, mites, electromagnetism, even the infrasound the giant
windmills make, that sends the bats and raptors
to their deaths, all invention gone awry, hive after hive
suddenly empty, as if they'd all flown out less than purposefully, casually,
and somehow forgotten to come back, held up at the doctor's or the U-Haul
dealer's, swarms of them, hundreds, thousands vagabond
in some other landscape, or rising, *we shall meet them in the air,*
at the post office to mail a letter to a woman who might or might not be my
       love
because a rate change had caught me with insufficient postage

I had to wait, the clerk was preoccupied with a sort of crate
made of wire mesh, through which I could see bees, *Resistant* the clerk said
as she filled out the forms and sent them, registered parcel post, somewhere
else, only then did she sell me the stamp I needed,
or thought I needed, or hoped to need (there is a season
when one hopes to need), and I thought about what it would be like
to mail a crate of bees, *Resistant,* to my love, if I had a love, and have them
vanish en route, the mesh crate arriving dusty, empty, one or two
broken, desiccated bodies rattling lightly around inside, like seeds in a gourd,
or like a child you'll never have, that is, the possibility of that child, the rattling
blood of it, a different sort of vanishing, we would all like to believe
in the act, that Houdini was a man, only a man, as he proved in the moment
and by the precise circumstance of his death, and the fact of his body,
lifeless but extant, rattling around the arcade, the park, the amusement pier
of disturbing coincidences, while in Missouri another hobbyist beekeeper
walks out to her tomblike hives on a spring morning
to find nothing there, just boxes, empty boxes, a sort of game
a child might invent, this rapture, same sort of funny story
a child *will* invent, when shown a photograph, *This is the policeman,*
and this is the woman with two heads, and this, which looks like a modest
red house in a suburb, this is really the ghost of the bees,
a small ghost, a modest ghost, like the ghosts of the locusts and the elms,
not a ghost to trouble us, until (in the photograph) the house spreads its wings
and vanishes, as houses do, or as houses will when the rapture extends
to architecture, the god of small houses having, first, existed, and then wed
the bee god, so that we are left sleeping alone again, and out of doors, in spring,
as one more source of sweetness is subtracted from this world
and added to another, perhaps, as we would like to think, one of the
more comforting ideas, a sort of economics, a grand
accounting, until what angel of houses or of bees blows what trumpet,
and we fall as mountains upon the insects, devour them as seas,
scorch the houses as with fire, *we* become the ground that hollows beneath
them and the air they fly through, their wormwood star, as all the bees of
          heaven
watch from heaven and all the houses of heaven lean down
for a closer look, and the smoke drifts upward, and we are the smoke, we are
only the smoke, inside of which my neighbor walks, with his ducks, and sings,
and they follow, and my hive lazes, drowses as if they or it were dreaming
us, as if they or us were touchable, simple as a story, an explanation,

any fiction, as if they thought of us, or were praying, or were dancing, or were lonely, as if they could be, or would be, touched.

from *New England Review* and *Harper's Magazine*

J . E . W E I

In the Field

◇　◇　◇

The bungalow is empty now. The clock swings in silence. (I see Grampa taking me to the urine bucket on a mossy floor, where bamboo curtains moldered.) The bigger room of the first uncle is filled with webs; over there, the second uncle's smells dusty; the third room (used to be a pig sty), dumped, was built for the third uncle, now a monk in the mountains.

Outside the door, dogs hear the squeak. You ride me on the bike, like those mornings when we had shadows—don't be sad the rice paddies are full of weed. In the field, fireflies shine with your favorite stars; they are friends saying good-bye. They call out your name: Peace Pine. Peace Pine. It isn't far and let me walk with you—cross the bridge of orchids. So Long, my pine, So Long, my pine.

from *Sentence*

DARA WIER

Something for You Because You Have Been Gone

◇　◇　◇

What happens to us when you go away goes something
Like what happens to shoes in a dead man's closet.
Things inert without breath or breeze to stir them.
As if at the striking of a bell or the blow of a whistle
Or a shot from a pistol everything moving comes to a
Standstill. Quite some race this. Impossible to find
A decent seat. We thought about betting the farm
On who or what might make the first move. We
Were never 100% all there before, why would we want
To be that now? It looks like a struggle ensued where
The hair went down. Ah, look at where so many choose
To leave their skins behind. We passed along a few blankets,
An armful of unworn blouses. We passed you from hand
To hand and solemnly swore to unmention your name.

from *Open City*

TERENCE WINCH

Objects of Spiritual Significance

◇   ◇   ◇

People love to humiliate each other.
They are fools and liars, and will say or do
whatever it takes to advance themselves in the world.
They sit, one by one, on their barstools contemplating
the failures of others, nibbling every downfall.
The men are wearing invisible condoms, the women
squabbling over who gets the best stem cells.
Electronic clusters of meaningless data force us into positions
no one can defend. Immigrants deny they are in exile.
Indians believe in assembling reports on the transparency
of defeat. Scholars are a joke—they poke through
the remains of the expedition in search of self-justification.
We know how the universe will end: there will be weeping,
of course, contracts will be canceled, the sun will melt,
sweet young people will be fired for no reason, and language
will be packed into a baseball-size planet heavier
than earth and hurled into the nearest black hole.

from *The New York Quarterly*

The Darker Sooner

◊   ◊   ◊

Then came the darker sooner,
came the later lower.
We were no longer a sweeter-here
happily-ever-after. We were after ever.
We were farther and further.
More was the word we used for harder.
Lost was our standard-bearer.
Our gods were fallen faster,
and fallen larger.
The day was duller, duller
was disaster. Our charge was error.
Instead of leader we had louder,
instead of lover, never. And over this river
broke the winter's black weather.

from *32 Poems*

Coyote, with Mange

◊   ◊   ◊

Oh, Unreadable One, why
have you done this to your dumb creature?
Why have you chosen to punish the coyote

rummaging for chicken bones in the dung heap,
shucked the fur from his tail
and fashioned it into a scabby cane?

Why have you denuded his face,
tufted it, so that when he turns he looks
like a slow child unhinging his face in a smile?

The coyote shambles, crow-hops, keeps his head low,
and without fur, his now visible pizzle
is a sad red protuberance,

his hind legs the backward image
of a bandy-legged grandfather, stripped.
Why have you unhoused this wretch

from his one aesthetic virtue,
taken from him that which kept him
from burning in the sun like a man?

Why have you pushed him from his world into mine,
stopped him there and turned his ear
toward my warning shout?

from *Poetry*

From "A Jar of Balloons, or The Uncooked Rice"

◇   ◇   ◇

Pick the acrid colors out.
—Wallace Stevens

Have you ever had a haircut so bad
you cried? When you open the drawer
after having poured yourself a bowl of cereal
do you reach for a small or a large
spoon? How conscious are you of your
posture? Will you agree to let a lover use
your toothbrush? Which chemicals'
smells do you like? During which phase
of life did you acquire the bulk of your
friends? Have you ever quit a bad job
emphatically, ripped off a uniform or apron,
thrown the balled-up cloth at a superior,
then stomped off? Grey or gray? Who
most often terminates your telephone
conversations, you or the person to whom
you've been speaking? In your bad dreams
do you ever throw the slow motion
punch? Are you punctual? Is your signature
legible? Have you ever had a birthday go
uncelebrated? What's the largest TV set
you've ever lived with? Showers or baths?
How much cash do you like to carry?
Ever been knocked unconscious?
One large winter coat or layers? If you cross

paths with someone walking a dog, do you talk
first to the person or the dog? Do you eat
or give away pickles? What's the highest
floor on which you've ever lived?
Who is your most promiscuous friend?
Do you get jittery during airplane
turbulence? How jittery? Do you still drink
glasses of milk? How many people
have lived with you? How's your balance?
Have you ever ridden in a limousine?
What are the chances, would you say,
of you becoming, one day, the president
of anything? Greater than none?
When did you learn to write checks?
Can you accurately size up the square
footage in a room? What games do you play
with small children you meet (such as
faking snatching off their noses by poking
a thumb between fingers)? Where you live
is the night sky starry? How high
can you kick? Have you wasted
much thought as to what you'd do
were money suddenly no limitation?
Cake cones or sugar cones? Are you quick
with your wit or do comebacks tend
always to arrive hours later?
Do you keep your photos in albums or
shoeboxes? Are you handy? Do you
cross the street to avoid groups of young men
at night? Have you ever been a part
of one of these groups and watched others
cross streets as a result of you? Do you
match and ball socks or just dump them,
en masse, into the drawer? Do you
bisect your sevens with one of those
squiggly hyphens? Have you gravitated,
traditionally, toward the top or the bottom
bunk? Is it your tendency to order
the same dish over and over, or mix it up?
Are you easy or hard to shop with?

Is your bed up against a wall, or does it sit
in the center of a room, accessible
from both sides? Do you own any pieces
of monogrammed attire? Aisle or window
seat? When eating out, do you set
your knife atop your plate and change
hands? What's your favorite cuss word?
How long did you call your parents' home
your home? How are you at keeping track
of which acquaintances you've told which
thing that's happened to you?
Do you recycle? Do you think that
every Bic lighter you see, when in the hands
of a friend, likely once belonged to you?
How are you at not losing pens?
Are you good at putting together kits?
When a friend begins telling a story
he's already told you, do you let him go,
or let him know? When making a shooting-
yourself gesture, do you do the gun barrel
with two fingers or one? Do you insert
the finger-gun into your mouth or press it
to your temple? Do you cut up plastic six-
pack can holders so as to save fish? What
colors have you painted rooms? When
driving by cows do you give in to the urge
to moo? What is the most valuable (to you)
possession you've ever lost or had stolen?
Do you miss it? Would you often rather
just stay in the car? Do you always know
the day of the week? Are you ashamed,
like admitting you don't read the newspaper,
when you're way off mark (though, in truth,
the most you can be off is two days)?
What about dates? Do you find you have to ask
aloud every time you're at the bank
or when you're on the grocery store floor,
attempting to pick out milk?
Isn't it nice how willing people are
to tell you the date? Do you have

any "original" items in your home,
anything with a total production
limited to one? Are you accurate
at guessing people's weights and ages?
Do you take into consideration their
feelings when guessing? Can you fall
asleep on your own at the end of the day,
or do you need "help"? Look at your
fingernails: did you just stretch out all five
fingers, palm out, or did you fold your fingers
down over your inward-facing palm?
About what parts of life do you have
anxiety about having anxiety? Driving? Do
you have a system when it comes to
pockets, or do you blindly dump in
coins, lighter, iPod, phone, smokes, etc.
then fish around each time? Blue or black
pens? Chunky peanut butter or smooth?
When eating bananas, do you peel them
nude at the outset, or peel as you eat?
Do you tear into wrapped presents or
open them neatly with the spoken intent
to save the paper? Do you currently own
a phone with a cord? AM or FM radio?
In school, did you pack or buy lunch?
Have you ever made a scrapbook? What
famous landmarks have you found
especially disappointing? Which do you
(or would you) find more embarrassing:
crying in public by yourself on a bench
or laughing out loud in public by yourself
on a bench? Would you rather drive
or be driven? Ever just want to spit in
someone's face, though you actually really
like the person? Do you engage strangers
in conversations on airplanes? If no,
it's odd, isn't it, when the time comes
to accept peanut packets or order sodas
and you hear their voices? Ever wished
(if you are right-handed) that you could be

left-handed? Do you measure distance
in miles or minutes? Is there anything
that feels nicer touching the back
of the hand than a tassel? What
about gently blown breath? Are you
in bed at a similar time each night?
Do you imagine sleep as a kind of rising
(you are a basket being pulled gently up
in a hot air balloon) or as a kind of sinking
(you are a flat stone no longer skipping,
disappearing through layers of lake)? Can
you ice skate? Do you own a bathrobe?
Do you go to movies alone? When eating
out, do you prefer, in general, to face
the crowd or the wall? Are you a person
that has certain items that are unequivocally
yours (a coffee mug, a side of the bed,
a chair, a place at the table)? What names
have you thought to name children? How
many different bathrooms would you say
you use on a given day? Are there bathrooms
(not your own) that you consider a pleasure
to use, even look forward to using?
Are you shy? Do you save your receipts?
Have you ever made love outdoors?
Before throwing spaghetti into the pot,
do you break the bundle in half? Can you
recall a [bowel movement] that produced
the thought: "wow, this is the biggest and
best [bowel movement] of my life"? What
did you call bowel movements as a child?
How old were you when you learned
to read? Do you nap? Isn't stretching
something you always feel you should do
more of while you're doing it? Why must
we always draw a blank after entering
a record store? What's the strangest non-
food item you swallowed as a kid? Do you
use Post-it Notes? Are they still there,
those ascending horizontal lines that marked

your growth as a child up a wall or a door?
In how many cities and towns do you know
your way around? Can you describe to me
your most frequent freak-out fantasy, or
do the particulars of your situations vary
so that it's always a new table you're
overturning or bus window you're
punching out? Do you ride the bus?
How is your handshake? Can you ever
know for sure if it's too hard or too soft?
When at a museum do you like to walk
around by yourself or take the tour? Can
you recall how the moon looked the first time
you saw it through glasses (if you wear glasses)?
When cooking, do you eyeball or measure?
Do you buy low-fat products? In which
of these opposing clichés ("absence makes
the heart grow fonder" or "out of sight
out of mind") do you find more truth?
Do you go, each time, to the same barber
or hairstylist? When at the barber or
hairstylist, do you tend to talk about hair
or realize that people there must always talk
about hair? Was your Christmas tree
(if you had one as a child) fake or real?
What was it topped with, an angel
or a star? Have you ever purchased
an item with the secret intent
to return it? In which of your pockets
do you carry your wallet? Were you breast
or bottle fed? Can you write at all
with your opposite hand? Do audiences
affect your attempts to urinate
or parallel park? Do you rise to occasions
generally? Butter or margarine?
Do you bookmark or dog-ear your books?
How do you show love to what is yours,
by wearing it in or attempting
to keep it pristine? Do you not mind
fighting losing battles? When was

the last time you wrote a handwritten
letter that was not a greeting card?
Have you ever collected unemployment?
Do you check the dates on coins?
Did you play sports? If so, what
was your preferred number? Were you
a planned or unplanned pregnancy? Do you
save hangers from dry cleaners, amazed
that they're free? When pondering
what things are free, do you always
find yourself inhaling deeply through your nose,
newly aware that air is free? What actor(s)
could play you? Are you a fast dresser?
Do you like to be the one who holds
the tickets (for airplanes, movies, etc.)?
Do you trust others? What about
doctors? What is the worst ailment
you've ever been diagnosed with?
Have you ever been diagnosed
as something? How are you
at metabolizing shame? Where,
in your calendar year, have the birthdays
you celebrate tended to cluster?
April? If you went to church as a kid,
did you and your family sit
in the front or in the back?
What things have you been doing
when you've received news that a loved one
has passed on? Can you sleep
with socks on? Can people place
your place of birth by hearing your
accent? What would you try to save
in a fire? Do you wear non-winter hats?
Pulpy or pulp-less orange juice? Do you
always watch for the longest day
of the year and then miss it? Do you
miss lots of things you mean to see
or do? Events you meant to attend?
Picnics involving babies? Do you even
notice? Do you go to the gym?

What is your favorite kind of nut?
Do you remove shoes upon entering?
If no, are you annoyed when you walk
into someone else's home and find
a pile of shoes and a note? Does
walking on rattling street vents make you
anxious? Do you tell people when
you're ticked at them? How are you
at judging clouds of the metaphorical variety
at discerning those which will blow
over and those which will grow to take over
your sky? Is there anyone who likes washing
silverware? What celebrities have you met?
What is your method for dealing with coins?
Spend as you go? Hoard? Roll? Are you
a sucker for foreign accents? Do you
rearrange your furniture regularly? Do you
live in a place where furniture *can*
be rearranged, or is there really only one
logical place for everything? What gift or
gifts did you receive upon graduating
high school? Do you get mad when a drink
is handed across a bar to you with too much
ice? Mad enough to send it back? Do you
send meals back in restaurants or just
suffer through them? Are there multiple
languages in which you're fluent? Why
did you leave your hometown, if you did?
What are you usually doing when it
occurs to you to clip your toenails?
Can you drive stick? If no, do you
feel that this makes you inadequate?
How do you occupy your time when
in a waiting room or on a train? Books,
magazines, music, or just looking at people
then looking away? Ever French-kissed
the inside of your elbow? Do you live
in a place where tourists come? Are you
skilled at giving directions? Do you
own a record player? If so, have you

owned one all along? What celebrities
do people insist that you look just like?
Is the resemblance such that when you hear
"You know who you look just like?" and see
the person's finger begin to wag you can
supply the name or names yourself? Do
you supply the name or names yourself,
or give the person the pleasure of recognition?
Is your name such that it is frequently
mispronounced? Do you attempt to pronounce
foreign words correctly, such as calling
a crescent-shaped roll a *cwaSAHN*?
Do you like being an American (if you are one)?
Have you ever walked around carrying
a bouquet of flowers just because you like
the looks folks give you on the street?
Are you accurate in determining the ages
of children? What age do you consider
old? How has it changed? Ever just want
to yank the gun from a cop's holster?
Are you a good tipper? When receiving
bad service, are you inclined to think
("it happens") that the server is just having
an off day? Can you spell (without
looking it up) the word "hors d'oeuvre"?
Will you wait for a booth when a table
is available? Will you step out of a shower
to pee? When writing the number 2
do you loop the bottom? Surely at some point
you've worn the clothing of the opposite
sex? Have you ever lived in a room
lit by a bare lightbulb? If yes,
when you opened the door and tugged
that jump-back-upping beaded chain and
saw the items of your life in that dimness
did you find it gloriously romantic
or hilariously gloomy? If you don't live alone,
is it you or someone else who changes
lightbulbs? Are you a good speller?
What physical skills have you lost?

Can you still touch your toes? As a child
were you able to turn a cartwheel?
Are you hard on people? What is
the deepest water in which you've been
swimming? You root privately for loose plastic
drink lids, wind-blown and cartwheeling,
to stay up, to keep rolling and rolling,
don't you? Do you think grades in school
mattered? Can you identify flowers?
Can you identify artists by looking at paintings?
Do you eat the crusts of pizza, or only
when they're excellent or you're hungry?
Do you eat other people's crusts?
Do you cut the crusts off bread?
Are you a member anywhere,
of anything, as of a group of people
that meets at a certain time
and at a certain place? What do you
think about Communism? Can cans
of whipped cream last long in your fridge?
How is your self-control? How is
your cholesterol? Have you ever
spent a night in jail or been
in a physical altercation as an adult? Have
you been cheated on? How
did you handle it? If you could walk
onstage as the lead singer of any band
in any time period who would it be?
When no one is looking, will you stick
chewed gum to a chair or table bottom?
When no one is looking, will you do
really just about anything? What is
the most money you've ever found
on a sidewalk or a street? Can you tie
a tie? What about a bowtie? In which
stores have you ever imagined having
shopping sprees? How are you at Trivial
Pursuit? Crossword puzzles? Does making
a good list ever feel like an accomplishment
in itself? Do you clip coupons or mail in

rebates? What's your theory on why the Martini
glass is shaped the way it is? Do you like
animals? Do you find it beautiful when
sidewalks begin to freckle with rain? Seen
from a high window, is there anything
more lovely than when all at once umbrellas
blackly bloom? About what subject (other
than yourself) do you possess the most
knowledge? Do you say caddy-corner or
kitty-corner? Isn't it nice when a drinking
fountain is cold and with the right pressure,
when you push the metal button down
and up pipes a sweet cold glassy little arc
of water? Have you ever been on fire?
Your cuff or your hair? What is the worst
you've ever burned yourself? Can you sing?
Do you find you begin singing
along to songs you know always a bar or so
too early? About what things do you think
you're a snob? Which is snobbier,
ballet or opera? Poetry or croquet?
How about football, beer, and Buffalo wings
as a little group? How about cigarettes
and cities and streetlights and walking away
in a leather jacket? Do you use raincoats,
or umbrellas? Are your faucets tricky
to the point where were an out-of-towner
to use your shower, you'd feel the need
to give a tutorial? Are they trickly?
When dealing with a knot, are you more likely
to pass the knot to another, sigh and say,
"Can you get this?" or to take the knot
from another and say, "I can get this"?
Are you a take-charge type of person?
Are you good with jars? Have you ever
thrown away a crusted pan as opposed
to cleaning it? What is the most difficult
phone call you've ever had to make?
What is the most difficult test you've
ever taken? Do you prefer aiming

fans directly at your face or setting them on
oscillate so as to best relish that all-too-brief
rush of coolness? And when a fan turns away
to, say, rustle an unpaid bill on the end table
do you follow it with your face as far as you
can? Do you sit and patiently wait? How
important is it for you to have things to look
forward to? When did you cave in
and buy a cell phone? Do you mind
getting shots or having blood taken?
How many people have you called
your best friend? Does the number of beaches
you've been on exceed your fingers? Does
a sense of true self-worth feel like the light
from a lighthouse, a sudden enveloping
golden feeling that soon moves on, too fast
to chase? Who is your wealthiest relative?
Who is your poorest? Do you ever snort
when you laugh? How are you at building
fires? How about changing flat tires?
Till what age do you hope to live?
Have you found this has changed with time?
When eating Asian cuisine do you ask
for a fork? Do you bite or clip your nails?
Have you ever bitten someone with the goal
being to break skin? Did you like high school?
When walking or driving with a companion
in a place where your companion is familiar
and you are not, do you tend to pay
no attention whatsoever? Were you cruel
or the object of cruelty as a child? The object
of cruelty, right? Aren't children awful?
What's the longest you've ever consecutively
slept (not counting when you were sick)?

from *Sixth Finch*

DEAN YOUNG

Off the Hook Ode

◇　◇　◇

Even if the wine glass can't hold wine,
it looks in one piece. Such satisfaction
when we think we can fix something.
No need to make a long list of fuck-ups
and regrets, it'll look like everyone else's.
It's not like there's a shortage of explanations.
By the fourth day, the roses in the vase
are experts at falling apart but they were
experts before while they were still connected
to the dirt. So were the beetles. Maybe
only details matter: what the flames felt like
before you knew they were flames, bits
of the porous world, the words that made up
your intimate code. How have we gotten so snarled?
Sometimes thunder promises rain but it's wrong
and birds fly the wrong direction so why
should you worry you're turning into frost
in summer? Even the wind contradicts itself
and the one who thinks he has the most to say
is the one doing most of the not-talking
which isn't necessarily listening while
the other goes on in half-asleep defiance
so he gets the gist like brushing fingertips
on a monument conveys great bulk and weight
but look at it: the angel seems just alighted
to scourge twilight from the mind, let the body
fill with stone. Nothing can be fixed.

from *American Poetry Review*

Lime Light Blues

◇   ◇   ◇

I have been known
    to wear white shoes
beyond Labor Day.
    I can see through
doors & walls
    made of glass.
I'm in an anger
    encouragement class.
When I walk
    over the water
of parking lots
    car doors lock—
When I wander
    or enter the elevator
women snap
    their pocketbooks
shut, clutch
    their handbags close.
Plainclothes
    cops follow me in stores
asking me to holler
    if I need any help.
I can get a rise—
    am able to cause
patrolmen to stop
    & second look—
Any drugs in the trunk?
    Civilian teens

beg me for green,
      where to score
around here.
      When I dance,
which is often,
      the moon above me
wheels its disco lights—
      until there's a fight.
Crowds gather
      & wonder how
the spotlight sounds—
      like a body
being born, like the blare
      of car horns
as I cross
      the street unlooking,
slow. I know all
      a movie needs
is me
      shouting at the screen
from the balcony. From such
      heights I watch
the darkness gather.
      What pressure
my blood is under.

from *Tin House*

CONTRIBUTORS' NOTES AND COMMENTS

DICK ALLEN was born in Troy, New York, in 1939. After nearly forty years of teaching college creative writing and literature, he retired in 2001 in order to write poetry full-time. He has done that, publishing with Sarabande Books his sixth and seventh collections, *The Day Before: New Poems* (2003) and *Present Vanishing: Poems* (2008), which was awarded the 2009 Connecticut Book Award for Poetry. Allen has also completed a book-length rhymed epic journey poem, *The Neykhor,* based on *The Tibetan Book of the Dead,* and a book of poems fusing Chinese food and Chinese landscapes, *The Chinese Menu Poems.* When not writing, he and his wife, the poet L. N. Allen, roam the United States in a Honda Accord with nearly 200,000 miles on it.

Of "What You Have to Get Over," Allen writes, "I'm helplessly drawn to phrases that can be taken in more than one way, literally or metaphorically, so that they become like Op Art paintings. Here, the admonition first put me in mind of people crouched in bushes close to some border. But then the phrase also sounded like the advice of a teacher or psychologist trying to help someone forget some trauma. And since in many or most poems the 'you' is a stand-in for 'I,' the poem is also a self-admonition.

"From this point on (all poets have this experience) the sounds of the poem, the assonances and consonances, the rhythms, images dissolving into each other, carried the poem forward. What surprised me was how in this particular poem, stanzas lingered over the two particular words, *wend* and *yonder.* (Another thing that all poets know is that something must surprise them in the writing of the poem. This surprise must be of such a nature that it will forever remain in the poem, like a loose screw fallen somewhere, or the ghost of a lotus petal. Such lingering creates the kind of small eddies that can make even an overly didactic poem tolerable.)

"Urging on the border crosser, I was trying to rouse him from being resigned to having only a cart to push or an old river to work upon. Lest the poem drift too far back to an earlier century, I let the struggle cross one of those kinds of auto graveyards where so many B movies play out in gunfights. Finally, there's a reminder that—too bad—there are many who dreadfully oppose anyone escaping from what is (like the traditional romantic poet reputed to be always a potential refugee from reality). An escape may be the kind of success that shames and depresses those who look their whole lives yonder yet never take a step in Yonder's direction."

JOHN ASHBERY was born in Rochester, New York, in 1927. His *Notes from the Air: Selected Later Poems* (Ecco, 2007) won the 2008 Griffin International Prize for Poetry. *The Landscapist,* his collected translations of the poetry of Pierre Martory, was published in 2008 by Sheep Meadow Press in the United States and Carcanet in the United Kingdom. The Library of America published the first volume of his *Collected Poems* in fall 2008. His most recent collection is *Planisphere* (Ecco, 2009). He lives in New York City. He was the guest editor for *The Best American Poetry 1988.*

SANDRA BEASLEY was born in Fairfax, Virginia, in 1980. She is the author of *I Was the Jukebox* (W. W. Norton, 2010), winner of the Barnard Women Poets Prize, and *Theories of Falling* (New Issues Poetry & Prose, 2008), which received the New Issues Poetry Prize. Beasley lives in Washington, DC, where she freelances and serves on the board of the Writer's Center. Her nonfiction has been featured in the *Washington Post,* and her book *Don't Kill the Birthday Girl: Tales from an Allergic Life,* a memoir of food allergies, will be out from Crown in 2011.

Of "Unit of Measure," Beasley writes, "Anyone playing 'Twenty Questions' has asked 'Is it bigger than a breadbox?' Why a breadbox? Blame Steve Allen, who first used the question on a January 18, 1953, episode of *What's My Line?* He was serious, but the audience cracked up—making breadboxes the new reference point for three-dimensional size. Anything can become a 'unit of measure,' from a handful of sand to the foot of King Henry I; it's just a matter of right place, right time. So the question isn't 'why a capybara,' but 'why *not* a capybara?'

"This is one of several cameos made by animals in *I Was the Jukebox,* and each poem stays true to zoological and historical fact. With creatures like these roaming the earth, you don't need to embellish."

MARK BIBBINS was born in Albany, New York, in 1968. He lives in New York City, where he teaches in the graduate writing programs of The New School and Columbia University. He is the author of two books of poems, *The Dance of No Hard Feelings* (Copper Canyon Press, 2009) and the Lambda Award–winning *Sky Lounge*. He was the founding poetry editor of *LIT* magazine and a New York Foundation for the Arts fellow. His poems have appeared in *Poetry, The Paris Review, Boston Review, Conduit, Tin House,* and *jubilat,* as well as in several anthologies. He edits the poetry section of *The Awl.*

Of "The Devil You Don't," Bibbins writes: "If I wind up in hell, I suppose I'll need to get a job. Having this poem on my résumé could give me a leg up with the boss."

TODD BOSS was born in 1968 in Marshfield, Wisconsin. His debut poetry collection, *Yellowrocket* (W. W. Norton, 2008), was selected as an Honor Book by the Midwest Booksellers Association. *The Virginia Quarterly Review* awarded him the 2009 Emily Clark Balch Prize. His work has been syndicated on NPR and in Ted Kooser's *American Life in Poetry* column. His MFA is from the University of Alaska-Anchorage. Read (and hear) Todd's poems at toddbosspoet.com.

Of "My Dog Has No Nose," Boss writes: "This poem came to me while I was walking my dog, Molly. I was bumbling along, admiring the beauty of the world, when I realized I couldn't share that with her. She was only interested in those sensory impressions that her instincts could interpret. I wondered whether in fact we're not all limited in our capacity to see and reflect on the beauty of the world. And that caused me to put myself in my dog's place, relative to my own imagined Master, who must take a far more enlightened view of my world than I do."

FLEDA BROWN was born in Columbia, Missouri, in 1944. Her new book is *Driving with Dvořák* (University of Nebraska Press). Her most recent collection of poems, *Reunion* (University of Wisconsin Press, 2007), won the Felix Pollak Prize. The author of five previous collections of poems, she is professor emerita at the University of Delaware, where she taught for twenty-seven years and directed the Poets in the Schools program. She was poet laureate of Delaware from 2001 to 2007. She now lives in Traverse City, Michigan, and is on the faculty of the Rainier Writing Workshop, a low-residency MFA program in Tacoma, Washington.

Of "The Dead," Brown writes: "The water's really clear in northern Michigan—too clear, since the invasion of zebra mussels has nearly sucked the life out of it. So I'm on the dock and here's this dead fish several feet below me, clear as day. I start thinking about the advantages of just rotting, versus cremation. Even though I prefer to be cremated, I'm thinking what's so bad about transferring the energy back into the earth instead of dissipating it into fire? If we could just rot properly instead of being locked up in airtight containers. Then I started thinking about my mother. We were at the funeral parlor picking out a casket. There's a lot of baggage, so to speak, about this. My father's a tightwad. My poor mother, unable to stand up to him, never got to do anything she wanted to do, go anywhere she wanted to go, or buy anything without enduring my father's endless ranting and sardonic sighs. At least she could have an elegant coffin. Here we were, my father, my sisters, and I, looking over the outrageously priced, satin-lined airtight ones. I imagined mummified remains. For once I agreed with my father. How silly. How futile. 'Let's get the cheaper one,' I agreed. It looked okay, nice wood, but it had no inner protection. Naturally a few years later, the grave began to sink. My sisters and I don't live nearby, so we didn't know until it was a pretty obvious indentation. It was upsetting in the way that death itself upsets a person's sense of propriety. I called the cemetery office and they brought more dirt.

"The poem kept turning back toward dirt, toward worms. I prefer worms to abstraction. I prefer to think of my mother mingled in the soil to my mother sealed away, airtight. Then the more I let the image of dirt, of decay, carry me, the happier the poem became. I think it must be happy to allow oneself to pass all the way through the process, to fully allow not-feeling. Nothing in the way. After that the ducks came into the poem, of course."

ANNE CARSON was born in Toronto, Canada, in 1950, and teaches ancient Greek for a living. Her most recent publication is *NOX* (New Directions, 2010). Other books include *Glass, Irony and God, Men in the Off Hours* (Knopf, 2000), and *The Beauty of the Husband* (Knopf, 2001).

Carson writes: "'Wildly Constant' was written in the town of Stykkishólmur, Iceland, at an art installation called 'The Library of Water' built by Roni Horn. Formerly the town library, it contains waters from all the glaciers of Iceland. (Roni Horn built a new library for the displaced books.) Each water is contained in a glass pillar that reaches from floor to ceiling and reverberates with its own cold memories."

Tom Clark was born in Chicago, Illinois, in 1941 and educated at the University of Michigan, Cambridge University, and the University of Essex. He has worked variously as an editor (he was the poetry editor of *The Paris Review*), critic (*Los Angeles Times, San Francisco Chronicle*), and biographer (*The World of Damon Runyon,* Harper & Row, 1978; *Jack Kerouac,* Harcourt, 1984; *Charles Olson: The Allegory of a Poet's Life,* W. W. Norton, 1991; *Robert Creeley and the Genius of the American Common Place,* New Directions, 1993; *Edward Dorn: A World of Difference,* North Atlantic, 2002). Clark has written novels (*Who Is Sylvia?* Blue Wind, 1979; *The Exile of Céline,* Random House, 1987; *The Spell,* Black Sparrow, 2000) and essays (*The Poetry Beat,* University of Michigan, 1990; *Problems of Thought,* Skanky Possum/Effing, 2009). His many collections of poetry include *Stones* (Harper & Row, 1969), *Air* (Harper & Row, 1970), *When Things Get Tough on Easy Street* (Black Sparrow, 1974), *Sleepwalker's Fate* (Black Sparrow, 1992), *Junkets on a Sad Planet: Scenes from the Life of John Keats* (Black Sparrow, 1994), *Empire of Skin* (Black Sparrow, 1997), *Light and Shade* (Coffee House, 2006), and *The New World* (Libellum, 2009). A new book of poems, *Something in the Air* (Shearsman Books, UK), was published in 2010. He lives in Berkeley, California, with his wife and partner of forty-two years, Angelica Heinegg.

Clark writes: "Doctor Johnson defines *fidelity* as: honesty, veracity, faithful adherence. This poem would appear to concern itself with Johnson's third sense."

David Clewell was born in New Brunswick, New Jersey, in 1955 and teaches writing and literature at Webster University in St. Louis. He has published two book-length poems about twentieth-century American conspiracy and paranoia, as well as seven collections of poems—most recently, *The Low End of Higher Things* (University of Wisconsin Press, 2003). When not writing poems, Clewell is often lost somewhere in the outer reaches of the UFO phenomenon.

Of "This Poem Had Better Be about the World We Actually Live In," Clewell writes: "The poem's title came to me in a dream: Walt Whitman or W. C. Williams or Weldon Kees was in the audience at a (gulp) poetry reading. Whoever it was couldn't keep from sighing and growing audibly surlier as the night wore on. It's hard to remember exactly; maybe it was just me, turning one too many pages in the new issue of *Fill-In-Your-Favorite-Blank Quarterly.* In the less dreamy Big Picture, each of us is here for a galactic heartbeat at most. There's precious little time to learn names, but we have to try.

"Many years ago I worked as a weight-guesser at the Jersey shore, and I was pretty damn good; it's one of the few carnival-style operations that isn't rigged. My margin of error was two pounds high or low, and during my two-year stint I gave away very little of the store for guessing too far wrong. I'm still working toward that former-glory precision every time I write. This particular poem, by the way, comes in at less than an ounce of words on paper—but I'm guessing it's a cover for the so-often staggering weight of the world."

MICHAEL COLLIER was born in Phoenix, Arizona, in 1953. He is the author of five books of poems, including *Dark Wild Realm* (Houghton Mifflin, 2006). In 2009, he received an Award in Literature from the American Academy of Arts and Letters. He teaches in the creative writing program at the University of Maryland and is director of the Bread Loaf Writers' Conference.

Of "An Individual History," Collier writes: "My maternal grandmother, who was 'incurably' depressed and delusional, spent more than forty years of her life in private and state hospitals, until she passed away, close to ninety, in the late seventies. A number of years ago, through a series of coincidences, one of my sisters came into possession of her medical records from the Central State Hospital of Indiana, where she had been admitted as a patient in 1937. (In 1967, she was discharged into the care of a private facility, where she lived out the remainder of her life.) The medical records are primarily summaries of annual physicals the doctors and nurses at the hospital administered and as such they contain notations about the dosage of medicines she was taking and her general condition, i.e., 'Placed on iron and thorazine (50 mg. 4X a day). Up in a wheel chair. No weight on fractured leg.' They also record statements and delusional pronouncements she was apt to utter: 'There was a heritage invasion' or 'I changed my skin, my hair, and my weight all in one year.'

"Initially, I attempted to write a poem based on the transcriptions of my grandmother's medical records, hoping I might fashion something like a found poem, but I never discovered a satisfactory framework for organizing the medical notations or her poignant and disquieting statements. A couple of years ago, I read an essay about the history of psychotropic drugs and found that I responded viscerally to the sounds of the names of the various drugs and that their etymologies began sending off sparks of figurative possibilities. Shortly afterward, I started a poem that tried to incorporate as many of them as possible. Along the way, not only did my long-dead college roommate Jimmy O'Laughlin come into the poem, but at some point I realized this might be the avenue into the poem I'd been wanting to write about my grandmother, whose individual history might also speak to certain paranoid and delusional characteristics of our culture."

BILLY COLLINS was born in the French Hospital in New York City in 1941. He was an undergraduate at Holy Cross College and received his PhD from the University of California, Riverside. His books of poetry include *Ballistics* (Random House, 2008), *The Trouble with Poetry and Other Poems* (Random House, 2005), a collection of haiku titled *She Was Just Seventeen* (Modern Haiku Press, 2006), *Nine Horses* (Random House, 2002), *Sailing Alone Around the Room: New and Selected Poems* (Random House, 2001), *Picnic, Lightning* (University of Pittsburgh Press, 1998), *The Art of Drowning* (University of Pittsburgh Press, 1995), and *Questions About Angels* (William Morrow, 1991), which was selected for the National Poetry Series by Edward Hirsch and reprinted by the University of Pittsburgh Press in 1999. He is the editor of *Poetry 180: A Turning Back to Poetry* (Random House, 2003) and *180 More: Extraordinary Poems for Every Day* (Random House, 2005). He is a distinguished professor of English at Lehman College (City University of New York). A frequent contributor to and former guest editor of *The Best American Poetry* series, he was appointed United States Poet Laureate 2001–2003 and served as New York State Poet 2004–2006. He also edited *Bright Wings: An Anthology of Poems about Birds,* illustrated by David Sibley (Columbia University Press, 2010).

Of "Grave," Collins writes: "The habit of keeping a skull on your desk as a reminder of mortality—maybe with a quill sticking out of an eye hole—passed out of fashion long ago, but poets will always have the great outdoor memento mori of the cemetery to serve that purpose. The so-called graveyard school of poetry in eighteenth-century England, whose dean was Thomas Gray, officially recognized a gathering of tombstones as a setting conducive to morose thoughts and lamentations over the transitory nature of human life.

"A fuller sympathy with these poets occurred in me when I began to frequent the vast Woodlawn Cemetery in the Bronx, just north of my home campus at Lehman College. Here, the remains of Herman Melville, Bat Masterson, Admiral Farragut (under a tall stone mast), 'Fatty' Arbuckle, and other notables lie among more ordinary folk. The cemetery is the resting place of so many jazz figures it was hard not to imagine a celestial session that would feature Coleman Hawkins, Milt Jackson, Illinois Jacquet, Duke Ellington, King Oliver, and Miles Davis. My own talking to the buried began there with the impulse to say out loud every carved name as I passed by, but fuller discourse soon followed. Why let death end our end of a conversation? On his annual visit to the grave of a friend, a pal of mine tells him the best joke he has heard all year, and he works on the delivery. And whenever I stand at my parents' grave, I talk to them at length as if on the phone or at the dinner table.

"My mother was always quick with a compliment, and when I was a kid my father loved having me on, testing my gullibility with fanciful stories and gorgeous distortions of the truth. So here's the poem, borne of that, acknowledging her kindness and posthumously pulling the old man's leg."

DENNIS COOPER was born in Pasadena, California, in 1953. He is the author of *The George Miles Cycle,* an interconnected sequence of five novels that include *Closer* (1989), *Frisk* (1991), *Try* (1994), *Guide* (1997), and *Period* (2000), as well as the novels *My Loose Thread* (2002), *God Jr.* (2004), and *The Sluts* (2004). His six collections of poetry include *The Dream Police: Selected Poems 1969–1991* (Grove Press) and, most recently, *The Weaklings* (Alyson Books, 2010). He is the editor of the book series Little House on the Bowery, an imprint of Akashic Press, and a contributing editor of *Artforum* magazine. Since 2004, he has lived mostly in Paris, where he is involved in an ongoing collaboration with the French theater director Gisèle Vienne. Their fifth production, "This Is How You Will Disappear," premiered at the 2010 edition of the Festival d'Avignon and is touring Asia and Europe. He is completing his ninth novel and maintaining a popular blog: http://denniscooper-theweaklings.blogspot.com/.

Cooper writes: "The poem 'Ugly Man' came about in a curious way. For a while, I was doing an experiment on my blog whereby I posted select, sequential images from found pornographic narratives that I thought were particularly grim and melancholy. I would compose captions that attempted to give a voice to and elaborate on the porn's 'secret' emotional content. 'Ugly Man' began life as one of these posts. It was originally attached to a series of porn images wherein one of the models had a very bad skin condition that he was attempting unsuccessfully to hide via an almost terrifyingly dark suntan. My blog was later hacked and badly damaged, and, as a consequence, all the images that I had included in the posts were permanently deleted. In looking back through the denuded entries, I thought the paragraphs/stanzas that eventually became 'Ugly Man' were even sadder without their illustrations. So I excised them from the blog and, after a little fiddling, the poem was born."

KATE DANIELS was born in Richmond, Virginia, in 1953. She teaches in the English department and MFA program at Vanderbilt University in Nashville. Her books of poems are *The White Wave* (University of Pittsburgh Press, 1984), awarded the Agnes Lynch Starrett Prize; *The Niobe Poems* (Pittsburgh, 1988); *Four Testimonies* (Louisiana State University, 1998); and *A Walk in Victoria's Secret* (LSU, 2010), both published in the Southern Messenger Poets series. Daniels is the editor of *Out of Solitude: Selected Poems of Muriel Rukeyser* (TriQuarterly, 1992) and she recently completed a prose manuscript entitled "Slow Fuse of the Possible: On Poetry & Psychoanalysis."

Daniels writes: "'A Walk in Victoria's Secret' comes out of a four-year experience of old-time psychoanalysis (four days a week on the couch with a mostly silent cipher of a therapist) during which I noticed the intensely reciprocal nature of the cognitive states and peculiar language acts of the two different disciplines known as 'psychoanalysis' and 'poetry.'

"What I hoped to do in this poem was to suggest something about the similar states of reverie that characterize (at least in my case) the *dreaming into* the writing of a poem and the *free associating into* the shape of an analytic session. When I found the Freud quote, I felt ordained to write the poem!

"For the past several years, I have been teaching writing and holding workshops centering on the many rich connections between psychoanalysis and creative writing at the Washington [DC] Center for Psychoanalysis, and at other analytic institutes and communities. I am currently organizing a conference on the subject of writer's block at the Washington Center in February 2012. 'Slow Fuse of the Possible: On Poetry & Psychoanalysis,' written in a hybrid prose form, collects much of my thought on this fascinating subject.

"The action in 'A Walk in Victoria's Secret' takes place prior to a session of psychoanalysis. The Victoria of the title refers not only to the Victoria of the catalog and mall shop but also to the persona's grandmother."

PETER DAVIS was born in Ruston, Louisiana, in 1972, but he mostly grew up in Fort Wayne, Indiana. His first book of poetry is *Hitler's*

Mustache (2006); and he edited *Poet's Bookshelf: Contemporary Poets on Books That Shaped Their Art* (2005) and coedited a second volume of *Poet's Bookshelf* with Tom Koontz (2008), all from Barnwood Press. His second book of poetry is *Poetry! Poetry! Poetry!* (Bloof Books, 2010). His music project, *Short Hand,* is available (along with links to his writing and other work) at artisnecessary.com. With a sweet wife and two beautiful kids he lives in Muncie, Indiana, and teaches at Ball State University.

Davis writes: "These poems—from my book *Poetry! Poetry! Poetry!*— reflect my very shallow understanding of the idea of Radical Honesty. I saw a segment about it on PBS once. How that idea turned into the idea of poems that 'addressed' something or other isn't exactly mysterious. On the other hand, it's not entirely clear. But it happened, trust me. So there I found myself, just thinking and thinking about how not all poems are for all people."

TIM DLUGOS was born in Springfield, Massachusetts, in 1950. He was a prominent younger poet who was active in both the Mass Transit poetry scene in Washington, DC, in the early 1970s and New York's downtown literary scene in the late seventies and eighties. His books include *Je Suis Ein Americano* (Little Caesar Press, 1979), *Entre Nous* (Little Caesar, 1982), and *Strong Place* (Amethyst Press, 1992). He died of AIDS on December 3, 1990. In 1996, David Trinidad edited *Powerless,* Dlugos's selected poems, for High Risk Books. A comprehensive edition of Dlugos's poems, *A Fast Life: The Collected Poems of Tim Dlugos,* edited by Trinidad, is forthcoming from Nightboat Books.

David Trinidad on "Come in from the Rain": "Tim wrote this poem on November 3, 1988, shortly after moving from New York City to New Haven, Connecticut, where until his death two years later, he studied for the Episcopalian priesthood at Yale Divinity School. Like so many of Tim's poems, 'Come in from the Rain' is full of his boundless energy and his irrepressible charm. Who but Tim could relish both the 'mass-taste' trashiness of *I Dream of Jeannie, Trapper John, M.D.,* and *Barnaby Jones* and the kitschiness of tea 'in the grandma manner'—in manically hyphenated rhymed couplets—and make it all seem relevant, poignant."

DENISE DUHAMEL was born in Providence, Rhode Island, in 1961. Her most recent books are *Ka-Ching!* (University of Pittsburgh Press, 2009), *Two and Two* (Pittsburgh, 2005), *Mille et un Sentiments* (Firewheel,

2005), *Queen for a Day: Selected and New Poems* (Pittsburgh, 2001), *The Star-Spangled Banner* (Southern Illinois University Press, 1999), and *Kinky* (Orchises Press, 1997). A bilingual edition of her poems, *Afortunada de mí (Lucky Me)*, translated into Spanish by Dagmar Buchholz and David Gonzalez, came out in 2008 with Bartleby Editores (Madrid). She is an associate professor of English at Florida International University in Miami.

Duhamel writes: "I wrote many drafts of 'Play' before finally arriving at this non-punctuated free verse pattern. I was trying to get at the fluid nature of identity and perception, misunderstandings and misinterpretations."

THOMAS SAYERS ELLIS was born in Washington, DC, in 1963. He is the author of *The Maverick Room* (Graywolf Press, 2005), which won the John C. Zacharis First Book Award, and a recipient of a Whiting Writers' Award. His poems and photographs (see and hear poetryfoundation.org, DC Poetry Tour) have appeared in numerous journals and anthologies, including *American Poetry Review, Callaloo, The Best American Poetry* (1997 and 2001), and *The Nation*. Ellis is a contributing writer to *Waxpoetics* and *Poets & Writers*. He is also an assistant professor of writing at Sarah Lawrence College, a member of the Cave Canem faculty, and a faculty member of the Lesley University low-residency MFA program. He lives in Brooklyn, New York, and is working on *The Go-Go Book: People in the Pocket in Washington, DC*. A new collection of poems and photographs, *Skin, Inc.*, was recently published by Graywolf Press.

Ellis writes: "Pres-i-den-tial Black-ness: adj-noir. 1. Concerning the post of earned Negro power. 2. The mountainbottomtop of Colored credit. 3. Sermon not sonnet. 4. Paul Robeson's congregational chest, stuck out. 5. Superior not Equal. 6. Legislative Negritude (See Pigments by Leon Damas). 7. 'Tonight I don't fear any man!' MLK, Jr. 8. Post Whiteness, Poetic Just us.

"Out of rejection, out of 'keep on keeping on,' again comes continuance, continuance and possibility; I originally wrote 'Presidential Blackness' for *Poetry* for a section on manifestos, and both *Poetry* and I agreed that it wasn't about poetry enough to appear in the section, a good thing because I probably would not have written 'The New Perform-a-Form' (which did appear in the section) had *Poetry* accepted 'Presidential Blackness.' If nothing else, my creative process has taught me to accept failure (all forms of it), to try again and try again and try again. I think the poem is about (although I am constantly trying to escape 'about') cultural courage, and the belief in achievements beyond equality, and having to always prove you are equal in art and life. I also wanted to provide something of my own broken blueprint, a road map (if you will) of some of the repair-steps the aesthetic practice of Race Fearlessness might take were it, openly and freely, discussed and accepted onto the books, in the classroom, and at work in the workshops. We know it exists in 'the streets' (not Wall not Main) but it seems, all too often, that craft, the craft of poetry, is taught in ways that hide or erase practices whose chief tool and line are not made in the mode of restraint—which means less mouth, less running-off, less race (not racist) specific technical devices. Race Fearlessness is all about speaking when you write. Thinking is not enough for some of us. Some mouths must march. The appearance of this poem in these pages is dedicated to one of the deans of Detroit, Willie Williams, and he knows why. 'What's happening, Brother!'"

LYNN EMANUEL was born in Mt. Kisco, New York, in 1949. She holds an MFA from the University of Iowa, an MA from City College of New York, and a BA from Bennington College. She has taught at the Bread Loaf Writers' Conference, the Bennington Writers' Conference, and the Warren Wilson Program in Creative Writing. She directs the Pittsburgh Contemporary Writers' Series, which she founded. She is the author of four books of poetry: *Hotel Fiesta* (The University of Georgia Press, 1984), *The Dig* (The University of Illinois Press, 1992), *Then, Suddenly—* (The University of Pittsburgh Poetry Series, 1999), and the forthcoming *Noose and Hook* (The University of Pittsburgh Poetry Series, 2010). Her work has been featured in *The Best American Poetry* series and is included in *The Oxford Book of American Poetry*. She has been a poetry editor for the Pushcart Prize anthology, a member of the Literature Panel for the National Endowment for the Arts, and a judge for the National Book Awards. She has received the Eric Matthieu King Award from the Academy of American Poets, two National Endowment for the Arts Fellowships, and a National Poetry Series Award.

Of "Dear Final Journey," Emanuel writes: "Drafts of this poem go back twenty years to a period right after my father's funeral, when I was sequestered at the MacDowell Colony, sitting, sometimes lying, on the floor of my studio, weeping, and finding language inadequate to encompass grief. I felt burdened by an obligation to write an elegy and, at the same time, felt it an obscenity to write at all. In earlier drafts of this poem the black ship *was* my father. His dark absence filled my horizon.

"I rediscovered the poem last year while finishing my new book, *Noose and Hook*. As I read the poem, I realized how much it was inflected by D. H. Lawrence's 'Ship of Death,' which ends, 'Oh build your ship of death, oh build it! / for you will need it. / For the voyage of oblivion awaits you.' I was sixty when I found and reread my poem. My grief for my father's death had cooled and receded, my anxiety for my own mortality had advanced. Lawrence's surging bravado swarmed in my ears. I revised the poem, and here it is."

ELAINE EQUI was born in Oak Park, Illinois, in 1953. She has published five books with Coffee House Press. They include *Voice-Over* (1998), which won a San Francisco State Poetry Award; *The Cloud of Knowable Things* (2003); and most recently, *Ripple Effect: New & Selected Poems* (2007), which was a finalist for the *Los Angeles Times* Book Award and on the short list for Canada's Griffin Poetry Prize. A new collection, *Click and Clone,* is forthcoming in 2011. She teaches at New York University and in the MFA programs at The New School and City College.

Of "What Is It About Hands?" Equi writes: "This poem was inspired by a book of photos that contained a lot of iconic images of hands. There were praying hands, laborers' hands, the hands of a mother soothing a child, etc. Since hands have always been an important signifier for visual artists, I began to wonder what might happen if a writer paid them the same kind of attention. At first, the idea didn't seem to translate too well, but as I went on exploring it, a rather amusing memory came back to me. I once did have a mannequin's hand that for some unknown reason, a friend of mine stole, and it upset me greatly at the time."

JILL ALEXANDER ESSBAUM was born in Bay City, Texas, in 1971. Her publications include the full-length collections *Heaven* (University Press of New England, 2000), *Harlot* (No Tell Books, 2007), and *Necropolis* (NeoNuma Arts, 2008), as well as the chapbooks *Oh Forbidden* (Pecan Grove Press, 2005) and a single-poem chapbook, *The Devastation* (Cooper Dillon Books, 2009). Winner of the 1999 Bakeless Prize in poetry and a former National Endowment for the Arts literature grant recipient, Jill currently resides in Austin, Texas. She teaches in the University of California, Riverside, Palm Desert Low Residency MFA program.

Of "Apologia," Essbaum writes: "'Christ forgive me everything' is my most sincere prayer. I pray it fervently and frequently. I hope I pray it fervently and frequently enough."

B. H. FAIRCHILD was born in Houston, Texas, on October 17, 1942. He grew up in small towns in the oil fields of west Texas, Oklahoma, and southwestern Kansas, and currently teaches poetry at Claremont Graduate University. He has received fellowships and grants from the National Endowment for the Arts and the Guggenheim, Rockefeller, and Lannan foundations. His fourth book of poems, *Early Occult Memory Systems of the Lower Midwest* (W. W. Norton, 2002), received the National Book Critics Circle Award, the Gold Medal of the California Book Awards, and the Bobbitt Prize from the Library of Congress. *"On the Waterfront"* appears in *Usher* (W. W. Norton, 2009).

Fairchild writes: "I worked as a movie usher in high school and college, and in this poem I am approximately fourteen years old and at that stage in adolescence where I have absolutely no sense of self-identity though I certainly hunger for one. However, Mrs. Pierce, living alone for forty-odd years, must have had about as profound an understanding of *'Nosce te ipsum'* as anyone possibly can.

"I had never seen live theater and had no awareness of film as 'art,' but *On the Waterfront* affected me so deeply that I am still haunted by it."

VIEVEE FRANCIS was born in San Angelo, Texas, in 1963. Her first collection of poems, *Blue-Tail Fly,* was published by Wayne State University Press in 2006. In 2009 she received a Rona Jaffe Foundation Writer's Award and completed her MFA at the University of Michigan, where she was also the 2009/2010 poet-in-residence for the Alice Lloyd Hall Scholars Program. A Cave Canem Fellow, she makes her home in the metropolitan Detroit area, where she and her husband, the poet Matthew Scott Olzmann, teach and mentor youth and young adults through the InsideOut Literary Arts Project and independent classes.

Francis writes: " 'Smoke under the Bale,' from my manuscript 'Horse in the Dark,' is an attempt to negotiate personal history and collective history, stereotype and myth. Here is a brief measure of not the beast within, but of the human within that must battle the beast without, the beast that others may take us for. What clearer evidence of our ultimate humanity than the roiling of language that reveals us, that insists upon our *presence.*"

LOUISE GLÜCK was born in New York City in 1943. She is the Rosenkranz Writer in Residence at Yale University. Her eleventh book of poetry, *A Village Life,* was published by Farrar, Straus and Giroux in

2009. She has won the Bollingen Prize and the Pulitzer Prize, was United States poet laureate, and has served since 2003 as the judge of the Yale Series of Younger Poets. She was the guest editor of *The Best American Poetry 1993*.

ALBERT GOLDBARTH was born in Chicago, Illinois, in 1948 and has lived in Wichita, Kansas, for more than two decades. His books have twice received the National Book Critics Circle Award and he is the current recipient of the Poetry Foundation Mark Twain Award. His most recent collection is *To Be Read in 500 Years* from Graywolf Press, which will also publish *Everyday People* early in 2012. His fingers have never touched a computer keyboard.

Goldbarth writes: "I always hope that my poems stand independent of any outside commentary, and for the right reader will be more interesting than any outside commentary could be. That remains true for 'What's Left.'"

AMY GLYNN GREACEN was born in 1972, raised in the San Francisco Bay Area, and educated at Mount Holyoke College and Lancaster University, England. Her poems have appeared in a number of journals and anthologies, most recently in *Sewanee Theological Review* and *The New Criterion*. A four-time alumna of the Sewanee Writers' Conference, she is also a novelist and essayist, and writes a regular column on edible landscaping and garden-to-table eating for examiner.com. She lives in the Bay Area with her husband and two daughters.

Of "Namaskar," Greacen writes: "I wrote the first draft of this poem in 1992, and presented it in the Glascock Poetry competition, where I represented my alma mater, Mount Holyoke College. (I lost.) I am generally quite a slow writer, and it often takes many years for me to arrive at the mature version of a poem—this one went through half a dozen iterations over almost fifteen years, and bears almost no discernible relationship to its original draft.

"Because I am fascinated by form and the various funny metalanguages it can speak in a poem, I've always found a natural ars poetica in the practice of yoga. In each, there's a common notion that formal contortions can be a path to insights you wouldn't reach in a more 'natural' posture. As hard as it can be to define art, most of us can probably agree that the heart of it is opportunity arising from constraint. And if you can get there without a pulled hamstring, so much the better."

SONIA GREENFIELD was born in Peekskill, New York, in 1970. She now teaches English at Cascadia Community College in Bothell, Washington, after working many lucrative years in the restaurant industry. She was waiting for her ship to come in but decided to swim for it instead. Her poems have appeared in the *Cimarron Review, Cream City Review,* and *Meridian,* although the birth of her son is her best work so far.

Of "Passing the Barnyard Graveyard," Greenfield writes: "My husband and I moved to the woods of Kent, Connecticut, to be near family for the birth of our first child. To walk around the block in this neighborhood is to take a three-mile journey. On such a journey one can pass the farm that abuts the Kent Hollow Cemetery, which is old and crumbling in the appropriate New England manner. The formal aspects of the poem were probably born from my obsession with writing pregnancy limericks, which are pretty rigorous in rhyme and meter. The narrative of the poem is true. I sang loudly at the farm animals because if they could complain, I wouldn't have understood them anyway."

KELLE GROOM was born in Brockton, Massachusetts, in 1961. She spent most of her childhood in coastal towns, growing up on Cape Cod and in Hawaii, Florida, and Spain. She has published three books of poetry: *Five Kingdoms* (Anhinga Press, 2010), *Luckily,* a Florida Book Award winner (Anhinga, 2006), and *Underwater City* (University of Florida, 2004). She is grants and communications manager for Atlantic Center for the Arts, an artists-in-residence facility in New Smyrna Beach, Florida.

Groom writes: "I found the silver print photograph in 'Oh dont' when I happened on an exhibition, *The Perfect Medium: Photography and the Occult,* at the Metropolitan Museum of Art in 2004. An exhibit of spirit photography, it included the three images of spirit writing that appear in the poem. The medium was still so new—photography just born in 1839—and the photograph in the title taken in 1874. It was almost like magic. The letters in 'Oh don[']t' looked as though they had been written in luminescent chalk, apostrophe missing. It's a plea, but the ambiguity of the request makes it impossible to know what to do (or to stop doing). The 'red in the sky, red in the table' are images from Chagall's painting *The Lovers,* with its apparitional couple. 'Oh dont' is a love poem, and this photograph opened the door to it."

GABRIEL GUDDING, born on Bloomsday, 1966, in Anoka, Minnesota, is a poet, essayist, and translator, whose recent work explores the sociology of literary consecration, the ethics and aesthetics of embodied cognition, and the social epistemology of calendars and clocks since the industrial revolution. He is an associate professor of English at Illinois State University, where he has taught since 2002. His poems and essays have been translated into French, Danish, Vietnamese, and Spanish. He is the author of *Rhode Island Notebook* (Dalkey Archive Press, 2007) and *A Defense of Poetry* (Pitt Poetry Series, 2002).

Gudding writes: "'And What, Friends, Is Called a Road' is the prologue to my second book, *Rhode Island Notebook,* a 436-page poem handwritten in my car on the highways between Normal, Illinois, and Providence, Rhode Island. I wrote in large-format sketchpads placed on the passenger seat of my Toyota Echo during twenty-six round-trips driven from 2002 to 2005. As a travelogue the book in its largest dimension is essentially a meditation on American violence and unsettledness, a chronicle of the run-up to war in Iraq and a study on sorrow, but it is also the story of a family falling apart. The book is dedicated to my daughter Clio. Though a long poem, the book is interlarded with mixed genre elements, including a few treatises (one on dung, another on literary narcissism) and several essays, including little disquisitions on vipassana meditation, Whitman, C. S. Peirce, and Nancy Reagan."

KIMIKO HAHN was born in the suburbs of New York in 1955. As an undergraduate, she double-majored in East Asian literature and English/ creative writing at the University of Iowa and later attended graduate school at Columbia University to study Japanese literature. She is a distinguished professor in the MFA program at Queens College, the City University of New York. Her collections of poetry are *Toxic Flora* (W. W. Norton, 2010), *The Narrow Road to the Interior* (Norton, 2006), *The Artist's Daughter* (Norton, 2002), *Mosquito and Ant* (Norton, 1999), *Volatile* (Hanging Loose Press, 1998), *The Unbearable Heart* (Kaya Productions, 1995), *Earshot* (Hanging Loose Press, 1992), and *Air Pocket* (Hanging Loose Press, 1989). *A Field Guide to the Intractable* is a chapbook arranged in the manner of a journal (Small Anchor Press, 2009).

Of *"The Poetic Memoirs of Lady Daibu,"* Hahn writes: "About seven years ago, inspired by Eavan Boland's 'Quarantine,' I began a series of love poems, dealing not only with romance but love for family and friends. I aimed to use outside material and/or stolen phrases to trigger each piece. I ended up with about a dozen that used literary allusions, some from the West and others from Japan and Japanese genres like the 'poetic diary.' (Others took a different direction entirely, drawing on material from the science section of *The New York Times.* These became my new book, *Toxic Flora.*)

"*The Poetic Memoirs of Lady Daibu* (Stanford University Press, 1980), by the way, was translated by Phillip Tudor Harries and is considered a minor work of twelfth-century Japan. Typical of the poetic diary, it is structured around a collection of poems written to put an event or a remembrance into relief. This genre has been a great influence on me, especially for *The Narrow Road to the Interior,* a collection of over ten years' worth of such hybrid pieces.

"While '*The Poetic Memoirs of Lady Daibu*' may seem to be about a relationship between family members, in my mind meaning is generated from the line 'scraps of allusions tucked between pages': that is, how we correspond with the past in a greater sense. I think."

BARBARA HAMBY was born in New Orleans in 1952 and was raised in Honolulu. She is married to the poet David Kirby, and they live in Tallahassee, Florida, and teach at Florida State University, which has a fantastic Study Abroad program that allows them to live in exotic places on a regular basis. Her most recent book is *All-Night Lingo Tango* (Pittsburgh, 2009). Her first book, *Delirium* (North Texas, 1994), won the Vassar Miller Prize, the Kate Tufts Award, and the Poetry Society of America's Norma Farber First Book Prize. Her book of stories, *Lester Higata's 20th Century,* won the 2010 Iowa Short Fiction Prize. She and David Kirby have edited an anthology of poetry, *Seriously Funny* (University of Georgia Press, 2010).

Hamby writes: "These poems are from a twenty-six-poem sequence of abecedarian sonnets at the center of *All-Night Lingo Tango.* Each poem begins with a different letter of the alphabet, and the first line ends with the next letter and so on throughout the poem. There is one poem for every letter of the alphabet. Although each poem has only thirteen lines, I decided to call them sonnets because in my heart of hearts I felt they were sonnets.

"I started working on this sequence in Florence in fall 2005. I was taking an intensive language class—four hours a day, five days a week—and something popped. I was probably driving new neural pathways through my brain—all those Italian verbs—and I'd rush home after class and start writing. My husband would come home for lunch and I'd be typing so furiously that he started calling out, 'Sylvia, are the children okay?' I finished the whole sequence in less than a month, which is unusual for me. I'm a very slow writer. It was as if I'd been possessed.

I certainly didn't have a plan, which is obvious when you look at the subject matter of the poems. I sometimes think of them as a snapshot of my mind at a certain point in time."

TERRANCE HAYES was born in Columbia, South Carolina, in 1971. His most recent poetry collection is *Lighthead* (Penguin, 2010). His other books are *Wind in a Box, Muscular Music,* and *Hip Logic.* He has received a Whiting Writers' Award, a National Endowment for the Arts Fellowship, and a Guggenheim Fellowship. He is a professor of creative writing at Carnegie Mellon University and lives in Pittsburgh, Pennsylvania.

Of "I Just Want to Look," Hayes writes: "The title is the poem's trigger. It's one of those refrains that can become, almost inadvertently, a mantra. 'I just want to look.' 'I just want to look.' It's uttered or confessed by voyeurs, bystanders, artists, and witnesses. Ultimately, I hope the poem argues that no 'looking' is totally detached; the line of sight is a tether. Subjects look back. Objects look back. There's a little bit of good and bad in it."

BOB HICOK was born in Grand Ledge, Michigan, in 1960. He is an associate professor of English at Virginia Tech. His most recent book is *Words for Empty and Words for Full* (University of Pittsburgh Press, 2010). His previous collection, *This Clumsy Living* (Pittsburgh, 2007), was awarded the Bobbitt Prize from the Library of Congress.

Of "The Cunning Optimism of Language," Hicok writes: "There's a theory that Amelia Earhart pulled the tag off her bed before she flew off into our imaginations. I believe this to be a more plausible explanation of her disappearance than engine failure, and it has the advantage of fitting the context of my current obligation, which is to write about the poem you may or may not have read in this anthology. I know many of us go straight to contributors' notes, and here I am in mine, not revealing anything of substance. In apology, I'll offer this valuable piece of information: there's a bacteria that eats plutonium. This amazes me, but I've never recovered from either the pinwheel or the whirligig. How they spin. How I spin. How every atom spins."

RODNEY JONES was born in Alabama in 1950. His eight books include *Transparent Gestures* (Houghton Mifflin, 1989), winner of the National Book Critics Circle Award; *Things That Happen Once* (Houghton Mifflin, 1996); *Elegy for the Southern Drawl* (Houghton Mifflin, 1999); and

Salvation Blues (Houghton Mifflin, 2006), winner of the Kingsley Tufts Prize. In 2010, Red Hydra Press will issue *Twelve Fables Set in The Shawnee Hills,* and in 2011, Houghton Mifflin Harcourt will publish *The Art of Heaven*. He teaches in the graduate writing program at Southern Illinois University, Carbondale.

Jones writes: "I'd just finished another poem called 'North Alabama Endtime' (now 'North Alabama Endtime 2') when I went to purchase a doodad. It was expensive and I complained about the tax. The salesman expressed the opinion that the government was evil; the individual, powerless; we were, in fact, being watched all the time. 'That seems unlikely,' I said. 'Do you have a cable television?' he asked. When I told him that I did, he said, 'Oh, they can see you.' A week or two later, my air conditioner stopped working. The man who came to repair it asked me, 'Why do you think it is that no president has ever died of cancer?' 'What do you mean?' I replied. 'I mean that they have a cure, but they're holding it back.' 'North Alabama Endtime' celebrates such conversations and the informing artistry of James Tate and Eudora Welty."

Born in Los Angeles in 1975, MICHAELA KAHN grew up in the amnesiac landscape of Southern California, seeking out pockets of wildness (a creek, a black walnut tree, the eternal return of jacaranda blooms) to hold on to in a bulldozed world. She was inspired to be a writer by her mother and grandfather (both writers) and her grandmother, who told fantastical bedtime stories. After obtaining her MFA in poetry at Naropa University, she worked as a temp, secretary, teacher, grocery clerk, editor, and canvasser, before two artist residencies allowed her and her husband, the writer Christien Gholson, to write full-time. Together they have lived (among other places) in an adobe apartment in Santa Fe, New Mexico; at 8,200 feet in the Rocky Mountains; in a crumbling old dairy barn in Wisconsin; in a one-hundred-year-old church in Pennsylvania; in a tent in Utah; and in a home with ten cats in Woodstock, New York. They now live in Swansea, Wales, where Michaela is working on her PhD in creative writing.

Of "If I ring my body like a bell of coins . . ." Kahn writes: "The bombs falling on Afghanistan in my poem are falling now, January 2010, 3,500 miles away from where I write these notes, sitting in my flat on the cusp of the sea in Wales. And they were falling in October, 2001, when I wrote the first draft of this poem, in the mild autumn of Sacramento, California, eight years ago. In that time there have been two presidents, an economic crash, countless marches, climate summits, other wars, and still the bombs are falling. In that time 12,000 to 30,000 Afghan civilians have died—not including those whose deaths came from the hunger, disease, and displacement of war.

"Everything is connected. In a quiet rice valley the smoke of the fall burn can be the smoke of a bombed school 6,500 miles away. What we bury returns. Through time, through earth, through our children. What returns fits in the palm of a hand, it ignites, it trembles, it smells of salt. It tells us the story of who we are."

BRIGIT PEGEEN KELLY was born in Palo Alto, California, in 1951. She has taught for the past twenty years at the University of Illinois at Urbana-Champaign. Her three books of poetry, published with BOA Editions, Ltd., are *To the Place of Trumpets* (1988*), Song* (1995), and *The Orchard* (2004).

CORINNE LEE was born in Lawrence, Kansas, in 1961. She teaches art and creative writing. Her book *PYX* won the National Poetry Series competition and was published by Penguin in 2005. Lee is a master naturalist for the state of Texas. She lives on seven acres in the Texas Hill Country with her husband, children, and an ever-changing assortment of animals ranging from chuck-will's-widows to vinegaroons.

Lee writes: "Beginning in 2006, my health collapsed, reaching a nadir with surgery to remove stage 3 cells last year. I read a folk art book during that period called *The Bird of Self-Knowledge.* The painting on its cover captured my bewilderment: a long-necked crane grew from a man's forehead, twisted backward, clasped his nose between its beak, and stared into his eyes with fierce yet unknowable certainty. Duly inspired, I began writing *Birds of Self-Knowledge* poems, more than one hundred in all, but never felt well enough to send any out—until the incomparable Brian Henry wrote, requesting a poetic sequence for *Verse.* The river to wellness can be stygian, so I still occasionally write a bird, but with increasing rarity as my health improves.

" 'Bobolink of Science Museums': Natural science museums—with roots in the Renaissance cabinet of curiosities/wonder room—smear boundaries, concurrently embalming and enlivening. Male bobolinks look like elderly scientists. 'Tanager of Carapace': A kushti is a sacred girdle for Zoroastrians. Rape has become such a popular war weapon that one UN official declared it is now 'probably . . . more dangerous to be a woman than a soldier in armed conflict.' I could respond to that horrific statement only with surrealism. The scarlet tanager appears more bloodred than human blood. 'Hawk of Moonstones': Ornithologists believe that hawks are one of the most intelligent birds. In India, the moonstone is thought to generate dreams. After surgery, I hallucinated the image of a beaked vagina speeding down the most delightful patriarchal construction of modern America: the highway. 'Moorhen of Dharma': Dharma can be difficult to contemplate when in pain; the moorhen, or 'skitty coot,' is a ridiculous-looking, weak bird. 'Pelican of Hokey Pokey': The majority of fish, a third of amphibians, a quarter of mammals, and one in eight birds are predicted to go extinct within our lifetimes. Pelicans can hold a huge quantity of seafood in their pouches and—after straining water out—swallow it all at once. They frequently access their preen glands. The hokey pokey is a nonsensical preschool dance. 'Shrike of Peptides': Shrikes impale prey on thorns, creating a food cache that they repeatedly return to, ripping off small pieces as necessary. I am both a Swiss and an American citizen, so the impact of global warming on glaciers is of acute concern. Swiss glaciers have, on a piecemeal basis, lost half their density in the past century. We are the shrike. The word peptide is derived from a Greek term meaning 'small digestibles'; a peptide also forms a type of chain, or bond. The 'find it here, in me' is meant to imply that our response to environmental catastrophe could perhaps begin in the individual—and in the distillation of imagination we call spirituality."

HAILEY LEITHAUSER was born in Baltimore, Maryland, in 1954. She received a BA in creative writing and a master's in library and information services, both from the University of Maryland. She lives in the Maryland suburbs of Washington, DC, and is, regrettably, unrelated to Brad.

Of "The Old Woman Gets Drunk with the Moon," Leithauser writes: "The original starting point for this poem was to write a villanelle with a drunk speaker, because I thought the repetition in a villanelle could sound like the rambling of a drunk circling back over and over to whatever emotional nonsense was stuck in their mind. I played with it for years, but I could never quite get it to cohere until one night lying in the dark in the wee hours of the morning, it came to me that the problem was the ABA rhyme scheme, that the speaker needed the exuberance of a faster, tipsier, happier AABB rhyme. The next morning I sat down at my computer and in two hours turned a decades-old dead-in-the-water villanelle into a working rondeau."

Dolly Lemke was born in 1983 to a modest family in Milwaukee, Wisconsin, where she has lived for most of her life attending college and working various tiresome service jobs. After five years of "figuring things out," she received a BA in English with a creative writing concentration from the University of Wisconsin–Milwaukee in 2007. She is now pursuing an MFA in poetry at Columbia College in Chicago, where she teaches freshman composition, acts as an advocate for first-year students, and works for the small feminist press Switchback Books.

Of "I never went to that movie at 12:45," Lemke writes: "I have ridiculous ritualistic tendencies. There have to be two tablespoons of creamer and one teaspoon of sugar in my coffee. It has to have that burnt creamy color to it. Otherwise I will search long and far for those ingredients. Sometimes at night I will lie awake in bed thinking about how badly I have to go to the bathroom but also how dark the walk to the bathroom is. I spend just as much of my loan checks on vintage clothes as I do on food. It's an impulse, a contained impulse. I have pretty much laid out all my faults, mistakes, and negative attributes for everyone to read. I read this poem at the *Columbia Poetry Review* release, which my mom attended because she is just so proud of her little monster, and everyone was shocked that I read this openly in front of her. I told them that none of this was news to her."

Maurice Manning was born in 1966 and is from Danville, Kentucky. He teaches at Indiana University and in the MFA program for writers at Warren Wilson College. His books include *Lawrence Booth's Book of Visions* (Yale University Press, 2001), *A Companion for Owls* (Harcourt, 2004), *Bucolics* (Harcourt, 2007), and *The Common Man* (Houghton Mifflin Harcourt, 2010). He lives in Bloomington, Indiana, and on his farm in Kentucky.

Of "A Man with a Rooster in His Dream," Manning writes: "I worked on this poem for about five years, and believe it or not, the basic dream of an old woman and a one-legged rooster was real. The old woman reminded me of my grandmother and my great-great-aunt, two very tough, good-humored, yet mysterious ladies. For me, there must be some spiritual attraction to this poem and its genesis; I've always felt the good women of my family are watching over me. Originally, the poem was in pentameter, back when I was enjoying the challenge of sustaining a narrative in blank verse, but the poem never felt right. Somewhere along the way, I 'translated' the poem into tetrameter (some of which is mighty loose) and that process strangely opened the poem, which seemed the right thing to do."

ADRIAN MATEJKA was born on an army base in Nüremberg, Germany, in 1971. His childhood was split between Frankfurt (Germany), Los Angeles, and Indianapolis. He is a graduate of Indiana University and the MFA program at Southern Illinois University Carbondale. For the past few years he has lived in Edwardsville, Illinois, with his wife, the poet Stacey Lynn Brown, and their daughter, in a house at the edge of a ravine. His first collection of poems, *The Devil's Garden,* won the 2002 Kinereth Gensler Award from Alice James Books. His second collection, *Mixology,* was chosen for the National Poetry Series and was published by Penguin Books in 2009. He teaches at Southern Illinois University Edwardsville.

Matejka writes: " 'Seven Days of Falling' is dedicated to Esbjörn Svensson (1964–2008) and was inspired by seeing the Esbjörn Svensson Trio at the Aladdin Theatre in Portland, Oregon, in 2006. That night, there weren't more than twenty of us in the audience, mostly from the Scandinavian peninsula. They were an enthusiastic posse, treating the Trio with the kind of aggressive hometown reverence usually reserved for Too $hort in Oakland.

" 'There are only oceans to catch me' is the best approximation of the feeling I got hearing the Trio's music, but it also illustrates the underlying mechanisms of the poem, which tries to reframe the discussion of race as one of hubris, rather than truth. It tries to redefine the expectations of skin the same way Esbjörn Svensson worked to reevaluate the possibilities of the piano.

"Svensson's repertoire of piano tricks was in full effect that night, and all around me, his skills were acknowledged in Norwegian or Swedish. I couldn't understand specifically what was said, but I got the point, because language and music are as symbiotic as magicians and white rabbits. The connections become most clear when we acknowledge that musicians do the same things poets do, only without trochees or consonants. We are both constantly trying to pull one another out of a hat."

SHANE MCCRAE was born in Portland, Oregon, in 1975. He is a student in the PhD program in English literature at the University of Iowa. He holds degrees from the University of Iowa Writers' Workshop and Harvard Law School. His chapbook, *One Neither One,* was published in 2009 by Octopus Books, and his first full-length book, *Mule,* will be published in the fall of 2010 by the Cleveland State University Poetry Center.

Of "Pietà," McCrae writes: "The figures of Mary and Jesus in Michelangelo's *Pietà* are so different in scale that, were they to stand next to each other, Mary would look like a giant—or Jesus would seem very, very small. As far as I know, this is because Michelangelo wanted the figures to form a cross, with Jesus's body laid across Mary's lap, and this would have been impossible without making Mary's lap disproportionately large. I wanted the poem to suggest Mary's continuing agency, despite all the uses her body has been put to by others."

JEFFREY MCDANIEL was born in Philadelphia, Pennsylvania, in 1967. He is the author of four books, most recently *The Endarkenment* (University of Pittsburgh Press, 2008), and a professor of creative writing at Sarah Lawrence College. He is a recipient of a National Endowment for the Arts fellowship and last appeared in *The Best American Poetry* in 1994.

Of "The Grudge," McDaniel writes: "The poem plays off the perverse pleasure we sometimes derive from indulging unpleasant emotions, which is perhaps one reason we return to them. I guess also present is the idea that, when we indulge these emotions, we are, in fact, feeding them, and that they have the capacity to grow.

"I had actually not read Blake's poem 'A Poison Tree' until after writing this poem. Many times we writers can feel like we're staking out new territory, but if we look hard enough, we usually see someone else's footprints. In Blake's poem, the nurtured resentment is successful: it bears fruit and destroys the 'frenemy.' In 'The Grudge,' the resentment only seduces and harms the speaker, which has been my personal experience with resentment. Hence the adage: pissing on your own leg and expecting someone else to get wet."

W. S. MERWIN was born in New York City in 1927. He was educated at Princeton. From 1949 to 1951 he worked as a tutor in France, Portugal, and Majorca, later earning his living by translating from the French, Spanish, Latin, and Portuguese. *A Mask for Janus,* Merwin's first volume of poems, was chosen by W. H. Auden as the 1952 volume in the Yale Series of Younger Poets. His recent collections, published by Copper Canyon Press, include *Migration: New & Selected Poems* (2005), recipient of the National Book Award; *Present Company* (2007); and *The Shadow of Sirius,* which received the Pulitzer Prize. Merwin was named U.S. Poet Laureate in 2010.

Of "Identity," Merwin writes: "I know virtually nothing about Hans Hoffmann except the vivid life, the penetrating eye of his painting of a hedgehog, which I have seen only on a postcard. I put the card in a safe place, but the hedgehog Hoffmann had places to go, and wandered off, taking with him such things as dates, origin, and so on, into his own life."

SARAH MURPHY was born in Lansing, Michigan, in 1969, and was raised on the central coast of California. She earned her MFA in poetry from the University of Oregon and her PhD in English from Indiana University. She lives in northeast Florida, where she is an assistant professor of English at Jacksonville University.

Murphy writes: " 'Letter to the Past after Long Silence' resulted from a fair amount of behind-the-scenes desperation, specifically my desperation to move forward from a series of poems in which the speaker ranted, boasted, preened, talked trash, rose in fury, threw gauntlets, and danced on her enemies' graves. For the life of me, I could not figure out how to calm her down, so, reaching back and borrowing from Yeats, I created the artifice of a 'long silence' during which she did not have contact with her nemeses and thus was forced into a more reflective mode. This artifice of time and distance allowed me to modulate her tone and rhetoric considerably; though it might seem a slight admission, saying 'you filled my lungs with summer' is a big step for this speaker!

"Lest I seem too disassociated from my poem and its speaker, I will also mention that the poem contains several autobiographical references. The trees and porch swing hail from my years in Bloomington, Indiana, where I spent one of the happiest periods of my adult life."

EILEEN MYLES was born in Cambridge, Massachusetts, in 1949 and is a professor emeritus at the University of California, San Diego. She was the Hugo writer at the University of Montana last spring. She writes about art, poetry, and culture for *Artforum, Bookforum, Parkett, Jacket,* and *Rain Taxi.* She lives in New York. Her latest book is *The Importance of Being Iceland* (essays, Semiotext(e), 2009). Her most recent book of poems, *Sorry, Tree,* appeared from Wave Books in 2007. *The Inferno,* a novel about being a poet, is out in the fall of 2010.

Of "The Perfect Faceless Fish," Myles writes: "I was traveling back from El Paso last summer ('09) when I got stuck in the airport for many hours. I was talking to Leopoldine on the phone and we had resisted cooking for each other so far in our relationship. She decided she would cook a fish in the coming week and asked which kind I liked. I said I preferred the fish be faceless and without scales. She said, oh I get it, a perfect faceless fish and that phrase sounded so beautiful to me and the fish then wound up dictating the whole airport, love, and general complexity of everything to me in my notebook that night."

CAMILLE NORTON was born on Christmas 1954 near Philadelphia, Pennsylvania. A late bloomer, she won the Grolier Prize in Poetry in 1982, graduated from the University of Massachusetts in 1983, waited tables, cleaned houses, and worked as a line cook. With Lou Robinson, she edited a collection of experimental writing, *Resurgent: New Writing by Women* (University of Illinois, 1991). She earned a PhD at Harvard in English and American literature and language in 1991. She is professor of English at the University of the Pacific, in Stockton, California. Her first book of poems, *Corruption,* was chosen in the 2004 National Poetry Series competition and was published by HarperCollins in 2005.

Of "The Prison Diary of Bartlett Yancey Malone," Norton writes: "Every meeting with a ghost deserves a story. My encounter with Bartlett Yancey Malone is no exception. In the spring of 2006 I was poet-in-residence at the Artist's House at Saint Mary's College, in Saint Mary's City, Maryland, the oldest 'continuous settlement' in the country. Unlike Baltimore, sister city to my native Philadelphia, the Eastern Shore of the Chesapeake Bay in Maryland belongs to 'the South.' The remnants of an earlier way of life were all around me, from the seventeenth century through the Civil War. One day, while driving a few miles from Saint Mary's to go swimming at Point Lookout State Beach, I passed an immense obelisk, flanked by a smaller obelisk, on the side of the road. The monuments were inscribed with the names of the thousands of Confederate soldiers who had died in Point Lookout Penitentiary between 1861 and 1864. The State Park, a refuge for boaters and campers, was built on the remains of a POW camp. In the center of the park, one found the simulacra of some Union army quarters, now used by campers. But in a nearby wood, where the prisoners lived in tents, I felt a heat, a sense of disease and pain lying along the earth. Young men had died in droves in this place. They died from dysentery, tuberculosis, and pneumonia. Many froze to death in their tents.

"I found an old historical account of the camp in the library, including some sections of Bartlett Yancey Malone's prison diary. I came to love Bartlett for his commitment to words and to learning. I loved his columns of homonyms, some of which I use in the poem, along with certain phrases from his diary. This poem grew out of my attempt to listen to him, to transcribe his voice. I wanted to give him something, if only this poem. Above all, I wanted to acknowledge, in a time of war in the Middle East, the dead around me."

ALICE NOTLEY was born in Bisbee, Arizona, in 1945, and grew up in Needles, California. Her most recent books are *Alma, or The Dead Women* (Granary, 2006), *Grave of Light, Selected Poems 1970–2005* (Wesleyan University Press, 2008), *In the Pines* (Penguin USA, 2007), and *Reason and Other Women* (Chax, 2010). She is the editor of *The Collected Poems of Ted Berrigan* (University of California Press, 2005), with coeditors Anselm and Edmund Berrigan. Notley lives and writes in Paris, France. She notoriously doesn't have another occupation.

Notley writes: "This segment is the opening of *Eurynome's Sandals,* a long poem I wrote in 2006. According to Robert Graves (in *The Greek Myths*) there is a Pelasgian creation myth in which Eurynome creates the cosmos by dancing it into existence. She is then encoiled by the cosmic snake Ophion and gives birth to the further details of everything. At the same time as I found this myth I was reading Boethius and got interested in the idea of time in the mind of God, with Eurynome as God. Thus the poem, with Eurynome as primal creative force and the filmmaker as time (he has a snakey tattoo on his torso). This is not to imply that he exists in her mind, it's more as if she is involved in simultaneous time and he is always trying to impose linear time, earth time. The time of the poem, though, is apocalyptic now.

"I wrote the poem in alternating blocks of poetry and prose in an attempt to make the two genres be almost coincident in effect. I thought it might be fun to tease the reader into not attending to whether she or he was reading poetry or prose at any given moment, by virtue of being absorbed in the story.

"I really enjoyed writing the work, but it didn't take long enough to write. It still hasn't found a publisher."

SHARON OLDS was born in San Francisco, California, in 1942. Her most recent books are *One Secret Thing* (Knopf, 2008) and *Strike Sparks: Selected Poems, 1980–2002*. She teaches at New York University and lives in New York City.

Olds offers this short biography of "Q":

"During the W. administration, I was looking at *The New York Times* one day, and felt sorry for the letter *q*—the qarrier of so much war news.

"Then I went to the dictionary, to find words in the *q* family.

"I knew it was going to be a punch-line poem—whether it worked or no—and I knew that was cheesy but could I be forgiven the shoq value for what it was trying to convey: if one feels sorry for a letter of the alphabet, how much more for a person, one of the hourly rising number of fatalities and severe injuries in an invasion so many Americans had been against? (And are we as helpless to affect policy as a piece of movable type being dropped into the composing stick?)

"When I include this poem in a reading, I feel a little mean—about to jump out and say Boo!—and hope the playfulness and the swerve and protest seem OK together.

"I was so happy when Paul Muldoon accepted 'Q' for *The New Yorker,* and Jenna Krajeski and I had a fun flurry of e-mails: Q & A became Q. & A.; quinoa lost its underline; the fact-checker found not 28 but 29 pages of *k*'s, and not 18 but 13 pages of *q*'s; and I was happy to get those 8's (infinities up on their hind legs) out of there, and the odd and sharp-pointed 3 and 9 in instead. Especially I was happy with the glorious long-tailed Q's *The New Yorker* has at hand—more devolved, more lemur.

"(And again, now, so happy to be between these covers in this company.)"

★　★　★

"Results of round-robin between the capital letters in the paragraphs above

> Tied for last place, with 1 each: B, D, E, J, M, O, P
> Tied for 5th place, with 2 each: K, T, W
> 4th place, with 3 each: N, Y
> 3rd place, with 4: Q
> 2nd place, with 5: A
> 1st place, with 11: I (surprise!)"

GREGORY PARDLO was born in Philadelphia, Pennsylvania, in 1968. He is a graduate of Rutgers University, Camden. As an undergraduate, he managed the small jazz club his grandfather owned in nearby Pennsauken, New Jersey. He received his MFA from New York University as a *New York Times* fellow in poetry in 2001. Pardlo is the author of *Totem,* winner of the 2007 APR/Honickman Prize, and translator of

Niels Lyngsoe's *Pencil of Rays and Spiked Mace* (Bookthug, 2004). He has received fellowships from the New York Foundation for the Arts, Cave Canem, the MacDowell Colony, and the National Endowment for the Arts. He serves as poetry book review editor of *Callaloo,* and is an assistant professor of creative writing at George Washington University. He divides his time between Washington, DC, and Brooklyn, where he and his family care for an old house.

Of "Written by Himself," Pardlo writes: "My grandmother collected glass and ceramic frogs on shelves not quite beyond my five-year-old reach. I made the frogs hop from the shelves to the floor where I staged elaborate performances. This infuriated my grandmother. I couldn't understand why she kept things around that were so fragile they couldn't be played with. I understand it now, of course. And I understand it clearly in the case of things that are dear to us. But I still can't help myself. I am addicted to the energy released when we split the twin atoms of the given and the made, or memory and experience. In 'Written by Himself,' I wanted to collage some of the unshakable images, and the tropes and rhetorical devices we find in slave narratives, and in other work in that tradition as well. These texts maintain our cultural memory as Americans and are dear to us. We tend not to 'play' with them for fear of dishonoring the history they represent. I hope to call attention to the ways in which this material can be transformed from the given to serve the broader scope of the imagination. I want to engage in a dynamic American history, shameful though some of it may be, rather than sit chastened as these images serve only the dour purposes of scholars and historians, or collect dust like the delicate tchotchkes on my grandmother's shelves. It seemed only natural that the poem would take as an anaphora the conventional first words of slave narratives: 'I was born.' "

LUCIA PERILLO was born in New York City in 1958. She has published five books of poetry, most recently *Inseminating the Elephant* (Copper Canyon, 2009) and a book of essays, *I've Heard the Vultures Singing* (Trinity University Press, 2008). She retired on disability in the year 2000 after teaching for a decade in the creative writing program at Southern Illinois University. In college she majored in wildlife management and has worked for the U.S. Wildlife Service and Mount Rainier National Park.

Perillo writes: "For a long time, on my desk, I kept a clipping about the hilarious procedure by which the elephant Chai was impregnated at the Seattle Zoo. The poem 'Inseminating the Elephant' was written after I read Jack Gilbert's fine book *Refusing Heaven*. In the back of my poem's mind are Gilbert's poems 'A Brief for the Defense' (which asserts: *We must have / the stubbornness to accept our gladness in the ruthless / furnace of this world*) and 'Metier' (which goes, in its entirety: *The Greek fishermen do not / play on the beach and I don't / write funny poems*). It was the slight dissonance between these two poems that launched me."

CARL PHILLIPS was born in 1959 in Everett, Washington. The author of ten books of poems, most recently *Speak Low* (Farrar, Straus and Giroux, 2009), he teaches at Washington University in St. Louis.

Of "Heaven and Earth," Phillips writes: "To be stripped of our restlessness might equal the peace that, presumably, some animals enjoy—a kind of oblivion that can pass for happiness. But is there no room for happiness within restlessness itself? It's an old enough question, one that I keep asking, on the page and—perhaps more dangerously, but without regret—off it."

ADRIENNE RICH was born in Baltimore, Maryland, in 1929. Following the selection in 1951 of her first volume, *A Change of World,* by W. H. Auden for the Yale Younger Poets Prize, her work evolved from closed forms to a poetics of change, rooted in a radical imagination and politics. Besides sixteen volumes of poetry, her prose works include *Of Woman Born: Motherhood as Experience and Institution* (1976, 1986); the essay collections *On Lies, Secrets and Silence* and *Blood, Bread and Poetry*; *What Is Found There: Notebooks on Poetry and Politics* (1993, 2003); *Arts of the Possible: Essays and Conversations* (2001); and *A Human Eye: Essays on Art in Society* (2009), all published by W. W. Norton. "Domain" will appear in *Tonight No Poetry Will Serve: Poems 2007–2010,* forthcoming from Norton. The title poem was included in *The Best American Poetry 2009.* Rich lives in California. She was guest editor of the 1996 edition of this anthology.

JAMES RICHARDSON was born in Bradenton, Florida, in 1950 and has for the past thirty years taught poetry at Princeton University. His most recent books are *Interglacial: New and Selected Poems and Aphorisms* (2004), a finalist for the National Book Critics Circle Award, *Vectors: Aphorisms and Ten-Second Essays* (2001), and *How Things Are* (2000). The fifty aphorisms of "Vectors 2.3" are among 170 included in *By the Numbers: Poems and Aphorisms* (Copper Canyon Press, 2010).

Richardson writes: "No one will ever write a novel by accident. Even a haiku takes time: you remember working on it and at least have the illusion of knowing how you did it. But if I say 'Pick a word' and you say one, where did it come from? You certainly don't say you 'wrote it' or 'created it'—more like you chose it, or it chose you. One-liners must be in the middle of that spectrum, as much accident as composition. Almost all proverbs and most of the jokes that make the rounds are anonymous: who came up with them, and how? I feel that way about some of my aphorisms, as if I couldn't claim authorship. I do anyway— 'Deem yourself inevitable and take credit for it,' says W. S. Merwin!— but I have a soft spot for the ones that sound most like proverbs written by no one, short and unsophisticated, their reference restricted to nature and household, faintly animist or fabulous or parabolic:

> Snakes cannot back up.
> Nothing dirtier than old soap.
> Water deepens where it has to wait.
> All stones are broken stones.
> Birds of prey don't sing."

J. ALLYN ROSSER was born in Bethlehem, Pennsylvania, in 1957. Her most recent collection of poems, *Foiled Again,* won the New Criterion Poetry Prize and was published by Ivan R. Dee in 2007. Her first collection, *Bright Moves,* won the Morse Poetry Prize (Northeastern University Press, 1990), and her second, *Misery Prefigured,* won the Crab Orchard Award and was published by Southern Illinois University Press in 2001. She has received fellowships from the National Endowment for the Arts, the Ohio Arts Council, and the Lannan Foundation. Rosser has taught at the University of Houston and the University of Michigan, and now teaches at Ohio University and edits *New Ohio Review.*

Of "Children's Children Speech," Rosser writes: "While I don't believe a poem is capable of converting anyone from reckless immorality to a moral viewpoint, I am convinced that poetry can deepen and recharge beliefs, even to the point of jump-starting us into further action. Amichai's 'The Diameter of the Bomb,' Szymborska's 'The End and the Beginning,' and Komunyakaa's 'Facing It' are to my mind among the few truly stirring political poems of this century because of their unobtrusive angles of approach. I hoped that the proleptic stance of 'Children's Children Speech' would help it slip past the reader's not-this-again, gimme-a-break radar. And while I'd never used the pantoum form before (it always struck me as of all forms the most absurdly unnatural), here it felt like the ideal vessel for conveying how we tend to spin our moral wheels in rhetorical mud."

JAMES SCHUYLER was born in Chicago, Illinois, in 1923. His books of poems include *Freely Espousing* (1969), *The Crystal Lithium* (1972), *Hymn to Life* (1974), *The Morning of the Poem* (1980), and *A Few Days* (1985). *The Morning of the Poem* received the Pulitzer Prize. Farrar, Straus and Giroux published both his *Collected Poems* and *Selected Poems*. A mainstay of the New York School of poets, Schuyler collaborated with John Ashbery on a novel (*A Nest of Ninnies*) and was coeditor of *Locus Solus* magazine. Like an expert draftsman who with three or four strokes can suggest a human face, Schuyler wrote "skinny poems"—pastoral in setting, exact in description, terse in expression—that could make a landscape come to life. In other poems, such as "Having My Say-So," Schuyler favored a conversational style and brought a touching intimacy and exuberance to the depiction of the erotic life. Schuyler died in 1991.

"Having My Say-So" is from a book of previously uncollected poems, *Other Flowers,* edited by James Meetze and Simon Pettet, from folders found in the Mandeville Special Collections Library at the University of California, San Diego. The poem is dated April 28, 1956, and was written about and presented to the painter John Button (1929–1982). This is Schuyler's fourth appearance in *The Best American Poetry* and the second time a posthumous poem was selected. For the 2001 volume, Robert Hass tapped "Along Overgrown Paths," which the series editor had unearthed in John Ashbery's archive at Harvard's Houghton Library.

TIM SEIBLES is a native of Philadelphia, born in 1955. He lives in Norfolk, Virginia, and teaches at Old Dominion University. In spring 2010, he was the poet-in-residence at Bucknell University in Lewisburg, Pennsylvania. A former National Endowment for the Arts fellow, he has been a workshop leader for Cave Canem, a retreat for African American writers established by Cornelius Eady and Toi Dericotte. Seibles is the author of several collections of poetry, including *Hurdy-Gurdy* (1992), *Hammerlock* (1999), and *Buffalo Head Solos* (2004). Each was released by Cleveland State University's Poetry Center Press. His next volume, *Fast Animal,* will be released in 2011 by the Poetry Center at CSU.

Of "Allison Wolff," Seibles writes: "At a certain point in your life, you realize that you are the sum total of your experiences. Lately, I've been trying to write poems that recount some pivotal moments of my early years. As a black kid who came of age during the late '60s and early '70s, I had to figure out a lot of things. It's easy to forget how little children know about the world(s) they inherit and what a mad scramble it takes to 'grow up.' At times I felt like I was swimming as hard as I could just to keep from drowning in the feelings and ideas of that period.

"As I was digging into my memory, the story that drives this poem leapt into my head. Looking at it now, I see that it contains many of the great anxiety-producing elements of *teenagehood:* issues of cultural identity, questions of one's appeal to the opposite sex, and the possibility of *romance* itself. It continues to amaze me that, while adulthood is often simply predictable, our lives began in a kind of breathtaking and scary wonderland where on any given day your mind could be completely blown."

DAVID SHAPIRO was born in Newark, New Jersey, in 1947 and spent his youth as a violinist and in the family string quartet. He was educated at Columbia and Cambridge universities. Many of the poems in his first book, *January,* which was published when he was eighteen, were written three to five years earlier. In 1962 Kenneth Koch awarded him the Gotham Book Mart Avant-Garde Poetry Award. His early books include *Poems from Deal* (Dutton, 1969), *A Man Holding an Acoustic Panel* (Dutton, 1971), and *The Page-Turner* (Liveright, 1973). More recent volumes, published by the Overlook Press, include *After a Lost Original* (1994) and *New and Selected Poems 1965–2006* (2007). He wrote the first monograph on Mondrian's flower studies for Abrams, the first book on John Ashbery (Columbia University Press, 1979), and the first study of Jim Dine's paintings and sculptures (Abrams). His poem "The Funeral of Jan Palach" inspired the monument to Palach dedicated by President Havel in Prague. His *Anthology of New York Poets,* edited collaboratively with Ron Padgett, was published by Random House in 1970.

Of "A Visit," Shapiro writes: "Fairfield Porter once asked me how I wrote the long poem 'The Devil's Trill Sonata,' and hesitatingly I answered that much derived from dreams and language in dreams. He replied, Oh that accounts for its dreamy quality! I accepted that as a rebuke and tried to emulate Fairfield's pluralist wisdom on figuration and abstraction, both of which he asserted. He also told me, in a walk a few weeks before he died, that if he could, he would end every sermon with these words: *Pay attention, pay attention to ultimate reality!* But he joked that John Ashbery had asked him what the word *ultimate* meant. We were walking on the beach near his home in Southampton on Main Street. I told him that I was convinced that John was a religious poet even of the 'outside of things,' as John had said of Ponge and Pasternak. *That's it,* cried a rejuvenated Fairfield. *It's not behind everything*—and gesturing to the morning waves—*it IS everything!* This was to me one of the characteristic strengths I looked to in poetry—a place where all the forces of a maximal poetics could take place.

"The poem 'A Visit' was a dream I put away, as if it bore the stigma of a waking dream. It took a few years before I was able to revise it minimally, to try to get rid of what Koch once called 'indigestible dream fragments.' In another dream, Fairfield appeared and told me that the world after this one was wonderful, as this one is, and that there are also no explanations, as in this one."

CHARLES SIMIC is a poet, essayist, and translator. He was born in Yugoslavia in 1938 and came to the United States in 1954. His first poems were published in 1959, when he was twenty-one. In 1961 he was drafted into the U.S. Army, and in 1966 he earned his bachelor's degree from New York University while working at night to cover the costs of tuition. Since 1967, he has published twenty books of his own poetry, seven books of essays, a memoir, and numerous books of translations of French, Serbian, Croatian, Macedonian, and Slovenian poetry. He has received the Pulitzer Prize, the Griffin Prize, the MacArthur Fellowship, and the Wallace Stevens Award. *The Voice at 3:00 A.M.,* a volume of his selected later and new poems, was published by Harcourt in 2003, and a new book of poems, *That Little Something,* appeared in 2009. Simic is an emeritus professor at the University of New Hampshire, where he has taught since 1973, and was the poet laureate of the United States from 2007 to 2008. He had two other new books in 2009: *Renegade* (Braziller) and *The Monster Loves His Labyrinth* (Copper Canyon Press), selections from notebooks. He was guest editor of *The Best American Poetry 1992.*

Simic writes: "I wrote 'Carrying on like a Crow' after not writing any poems for a year. Once I began again, I found myself extremely self-conscious and wary about trying to make sense of my experience of the world. The poem explains the reasons for feeling that way."

FRANK STANFORD, born in Mississippi in 1948, was a prolific poet who has been called one of the great voices of death. He wrote ten volumes of poetry and a collection of short stories: *The Singing Knives* (1971), *Ladies from Hell* (1974), *Field Talk* (1974), *Shade* (1975), *Arkansas Bench Stone* (1975), *Constant Stranger* (1976), *The Battlefield Where the Moon Says I Love You* (1977), *Crib Death* (1978), *You* (1979), *The Light the Dead See* (1991), and *Conditions Uncertain and Likely to Pass Away* (1990). Stanford worked as a land surveyor and spent most of his life in Arkansas. He died in 1978.

GERALD STERN was born in Pittsburgh, Pennsylvania, in 1925. He is the author of fifteen books of poetry, including *Save the Last Dance* (W. W. Norton, 2008) and *Everything Is Burning* (Norton, 2005). *This Time: New and Selected Poems* won the 1998 National Book Award. The paperback edition of his personal essays, titled *What I Can't Bear Losing,* was published in the fall of 2009 by Trinity University Press. Awarded the 2005 Wallace Stevens Award by the Academy of American Poets, he is currently a chancellor of the Academy of American Poets. He has retired from teaching at the University of Iowa Writers' Workshop. Norton published his *Early Collected Poems 1965–1992* in 2010.

Of "Stoop," Stern writes: "The central event of this poem, to the degree that there is an event, is a meeting I had—or probably had—twenty or thirty years ago at the Waverly Restaurant on Sixth Avenue in New York, near what used to be Balducci's, and the public library across the street, which once housed a women's prison. The meeting was probably burdensome, though, as I said in the poem, 'I was given to meetings / like that'—but my lifelong dream, dumb as it might be, was to be free of burdens. It still is; and thinking of burdens I obviously thought of the poor mule who spends a burdensome life. I have always identified with such a mule. The poem ends with the death of the mule (and me), as if remembering the Erie Canal song that has the line 'I know a mule and her name is Sal.' Molly is also a common name for mules. And I hope I'm forgiven for identifying such a stubborn animal with the 'she' of King Solomon's time, who was wise 'above rubies.'

"Of course that is my reading of the poem right now, February 4, 2010. What interests me most is that, in the poem, I am sitting on a stoop, eating boiled beef with horseradish, and I am wondering to myself whether the horseradish is white or red."

Born in Florida in 1967, STEPHEN CAMPBELL SUTHERLAND was schooled in the United States and England before studying philosophy and theology at Oxford. He has subsequently lived in Berlin, New York City,

West Africa, and Chiang Mai, Thailand, where he taught at the University. He works as a fine arts consultant and researcher in London.

JAMES TATE was born in Kansas City, Missouri, in 1943. His newest book is *The Ghost Soldiers* (Ecco/HarperCollins, 2008). He teaches in the MFA program for poets and writers at the University of Massachusetts, Amherst. He has won the Pulitzer Prize and the National Book Award. He was guest editor of *The Best American Poetry 1997*.

DAVID TRINIDAD was born in Los Angeles, California, in 1953. His books include *Plasticville* (2000), *Phoebe 2002: An Essay in Verse* (with Jeffery Conway and Lynn Crosbie, 2003), *The Late Show* (2007), and *By Myself* (with D. A. Powell, 2009), all published by Turtle Point Press. *Dear Prudence: New and Selected Poems* will be published by Turtle Point in fall 2011. Trinidad edited *A Fast Life: The Collected Poems of Tim Dlugos,* forthcoming from Nightboat Books. He lives in Chicago, teaches at Columbia College, and is coeditor of the journal *Court Green*.

Of "Black Telephone," Trinidad writes: "The actual telephone that inspired this poem is in an unwatchable Natalie Wood film from the early sixties, *Cash McCall.* There's a close-up of it at the beginning of the movie. But I had telephones on the brain; that's why it captivated me. I was in the middle of writing an essay about the telephone incident that precipitated the end of Sylvia Plath and Ted Hughes's marriage (Plath pulled the phone cord out of the wall when she intercepted a call from Assia Wevill, with whom Hughes was having an affair), and the way that incident reverberates in such poems as Plath's 'Words heard, by accident, over the phone' and 'The Fearful' (and even 'Daddy') and Hughes's 'Do Not Pick Up the Telephone.' Thus I was thinking about the telephone as a 'trauma object' (Catherine Bowman's term) and as an instrument of terror in movies like *Sorry, Wrong Number* and *Midnight Lace.* So deep was I into research about Plath and Hughes, I knew that their Devon telephone number, before Plath severed the connection in July 1962, was North Tawton 370; after it was reinstalled the following November, it changed to North Tawton 447. I was astounded to realize that Plath was without phone service when she wrote the bulk of her *Ariel* poems that October, a fact that explains, in part, the urgency of the work.

"Certain that Plath would have appreciated my attention to detail, I had to find out the model of her telephone. It would have been from the 700 series (706, to be exact), available in Britain from 1959 to 1967; 'subscribers' rented their phones from the General Post Office, and had to wait several months to have them 'fitted' by a GPO engineer. The interval, then, during which Plath was cut off from the rest of the world, which ironically helped facilitate her great poetic output. Of course once I knew the model, obsessiveness (or should I say fetishism) led me to Ruby Tuesday, a store in Shropshire that sells vintage telephones on eBay. From them I bought (for £65, plus another £30 for postage) an example of the very phone Sylvia angrily ripped from the wall. It sits here on my desk, magical by association, and beautiful (to my mind) in its shiny black obsolescence."

CHASE TWICHELL was born in New Haven, Connecticut, in 1950. She has published six books of poetry: *Dog Language* (2005), *The Snow Watcher* (1998), *The Ghost of Eden* (1995), *Perdido* (1991), *The Odds* (1985), and *Northern Spy* (1981). *Horses Where the Answers Should Have Been: New & Selected Poems* was published by Copper Canyon Press in 2010. She is the translator, with Tony K. Stewart, of *The Lover of God* by Rabindranath Tagore (Copper Canyon, 2003), and coeditor with Robin Behn of *The Practice of Poetry: Writing Exercises from Poets Who Teach* (HarperCollins, 2002). She has received fellowships from the National Endowment for the Arts, the Artists Foundation, the New Jersey State Council on the Arts, the John Simon Guggenheim Memorial Foundation, and the American Academy of Arts and Letters. After teaching for many years (Warren Wilson College, the University of Alabama, Goddard College, Hampshire College, and Princeton University), she left academe to start Ausable Press, a not-for-profit publisher of poetry, which was acquired by Copper Canyon Press in 2009. A student in the Mountains and Rivers Order at Zen Mountain Monastery, she lives in upstate New York with her husband, the novelist Russell Banks.

Twichell writes: "For years I've circled, in poems, the underlying subject of 'The Dark Rides.' I was unable to address it head-on for several reasons: the actual events were only half-remembered; the boundary between private and public became disturbingly porous in the telling; and most of all, how do you locate the truth and meaning of such a thing from the vantage of over fifty years? For decades I kept the secret hidden away, a dead seed, but it was stubborn, and eventually sprouted. 'The Dark Rides' is one of a large cluster of poems that look back at the trauma of childhood sexual improprieties (I was never physically injured) through the veils of memory and time. Poems are not nonfiction. Are they fiction, then? As I wrote in another poem,

What I know is a slur of memory,
fantasy, research, pure invention,
crime dramas, news, and witnesses
like the girl who liked to get high
and the one who was eventually
returned to her family unharmed.
The rest I made up."

JOHN UPDIKE was born in Shillington, Pennsylvania, in 1932. He received his BA from Harvard University in 1954, moved to New York, and began writing for *The New Yorker,* the magazine to which he would contribute stories, essays, reviews, poems, and "Talk of the Town" pieces for the rest of his life. But he resisted the lure of the city and moved to a quiet town near Boston. He became perhaps the most productive writer of his generation. He tended to his vocation as an artist with the dedication of a monk. Begun in 1959, and completed thirty years later, his quartet of novels centering upon Harry "Rabbit" Angstrom captures the changing American social landscape in the last half of the twentieth century. It is, in toto, a four-volume novel about the man that Updike could have been: a sensualist and an athlete, blue-collar in instinct, who likes the voice of Perry Como on his car radio as he drives away from home, escaping to nowhere. A technical tour de force, the four books are all told in the present tense.

Another alter ego was Henry Bech, the subject of three collections of stories in a more whimsical mode. The creation of Bech, a Jewish American writer who resembles an unbuttoned Bernard Malamud, allowed Updike to satirize the world of New York literary warfare that he managed to avoid. Before his final apotheosis as a Nobel laureate, Bech (who is "good in bed but impotent elsewhere") discards one mistress, acquires another, and figures out a way to kill selected critics through the mail with impunity. On top of everything else Updike was himself arguably the most versatile critic in the country. His collections of essays, *Hugging the Shore* (1983) foremost among them, reveal his remarkable range and subtle intelligence applied to all manner of things—to Kierkegaard, to theology, to painting, to golf, and of course to literature.

Updike's poems have always been underrated, yet he wrote as skillfully about Doris Day as about former girlfriends ("No More Access to Her Underpants"), *The Naked Ape,* a favorite popular singer, or the experience of a colonoscopy. "The idea of verse, of poetry, has always, during forty years spent primarily working in prose, stood at my elbow, as a standing invitation to the highest kind of verbal exercise—the most satisfying, the most archaic, the most elusive of critical control," he wrote. On his birthday in March 2002 he embarked on a sequence of unrhymed sonnets entitled *Endpoint*. The last group of these was written in the face of imminent death. Updike learned he had lung cancer in November 2008: "It seems that death has found / the portals it will enter by: my lungs, / pathetic oblong ghosts, one paler than / the other on the doctor's viewing screen." There follows a final flowering of poems that chronicle the world ("President Obama waits / downstairs to be unwrapped") as they look back at the past and prepare the author for his endpoint. The three sonnets chosen for this volume of *The Best American Poetry* salute some of the childhood friends, a "scant hundred" of them, who provided him with a lifelong "sufficiency of human types: beauty, / bully, hanger-on, natural, / twin and fatso—all a writer needs, all there in Shillington."

Updike died on January 27, 2009.—DL

DEREK WALCOTT was born in 1930 in the town of Castries in St. Lucia, one of the Windward Islands in the Lesser Antilles. After studying at St. Mary's College in his native island and at the University of the West Indies in Jamaica, Walcott moved to Trinidad in 1953. In 1959 he founded the Trinidad Theatre Workshop. He won the Nobel Prize in Literature in 1992. His books of poetry include *Another Life* (1973), *Sea Grapes* (1976), *The Star-Apple Kingdom* (1979), *The Fortunate Traveler* (1981), *Midsummer* (1984), *Collected Poems, 1948–1984* (1986), and *Omeros* (1990), a retelling of Homeric stories in a twentieth-century Caribbean setting. Several of Walcott's plays have been produced in the United States, and his first collection of essays, *What the Twilight Says,* was published by Farrar, Straus and Giroux in 1998. Walcott retired from teaching poetry and drama in the creative writing department at Boston University in 2007. His most recent collection of poems is *White Egrets* (Farrar, Straus and Giroux, 2010).

G. C. WALDREP was born in South Boston, Virginia, in 1968. He is the author of four collections of poems: *Goldbeater's Skin* (Center for Literary Publishing, 2003), winner of the Colorado Prize; *Disclamor* (BOA Editions, 2007); *Archicembalo* (Tupelo Press, 2009), winner of the Dorset Prize; and, with John Gallaher, *Your Father on the Train of Ghosts* (BOA Editions, forthcoming 2011). He was a 2007 National

Endowment for the Arts Fellow in Literature. He lives in Lewisburg, Pennsylvania, and teaches at Bucknell University.

Of "Their Faces Shall Be as Flames," Waldrep writes: "I wrote this poem in May 2007, when Colony Collapse Disorder and the sudden, drastic decline of the North American honeybee population were still terrifying mysteries. I had planted cosmos and zinnias in the yard—I lived then in a rambling Victorian house I'd bought in Mt. Vernon, Ohio—but they attracted no honeybees that spring and summer, none at all.

"The kernel or genesis of the poem was the idea that perhaps the bees had been raptured, in the evangelical Christian sense of that word. I drafted it swiftly, on the evening of the visit to the post office alluded to in the poem. The title of the poem is taken from Isaiah 13:8."

J. E. WEI was raised in Taiwan, where he was born in 1963. He received his PhD in American literature and creative writing at the State University of New York at Binghamton. His chapbook *The Quiet Hours* was published by Foothills (2002). He lives and works in Taiwan. His Chinese poems have been widely published in Taiwanese poetry magazines, including *Li Poetry, poch Poetry Quarterly, Contemporary Taiwanese Poetry Quarterly, Youth Literary, Qianqun Poetry,* and *Zhangmen Poetry.* Wei teaches writing and literature as an assistant professor at St. John's University and Tamkang University in Taipei. He is working on poetry projects about Minnesota and Andalucía in Spain, where he spent several years.

Of "In the Field," Wei writes: "When I was a child, I often visited my grandfather who lived in a bungalow in the country in southern Taiwan. He had lost my grandmother, and my uncles had all left home to work in Taipei. He had a rice paddy and we went there to irrigate the plants. The road to the field was zigzagging along with birds chirping in the trees. After working, we sat under the trees and took out our lunch boxes. The clouds floated on the hills where pineapples grew lavishly. After the meal, my grandfather would go to the small brook to pick up water lilies. From the wooden bridge, we saw beautiful water lilies, stretching their arms in the sound of the water. Our shadows, so small, floated in the limpid currents.

"My grandfather has a very ordinary name in Chinese—An Song—which means 'Peace Pine.' I saw him off one day in the field and never saw him again. Only in the dream can I see him standing like a pine. I dedicate this poem to my grandfather, who was not afraid of walking across the bridge to visit my mother and grandmother up there in the sky of endless blue."

DARA WIER was born in New Orleans, Louisiana, in 1949. She teaches at the University of Massachusetts Amherst, codirects the Juniper Initiative for Literary Arts and Action, and is on the permanent faculty of the Juniper Summer Writing Institute. Her newest book is *Selected Poems,* from Wave Books. Also from Wave are *Remnants of Hannah, Reverse Rapture,* and *Hat on a Pond.* Other books include *Voyages in English, All You Have in Common,* and *Blue for the Plough,* all from Carnegie Mellon University Press. Along with Guy Pettit and Emily Pettit she edits for Factory Hollow Press.

Wier writes: "Because we have the right, and maybe the obligation, to whisper to the dead in poems, 'Something for You Because You Have Been Gone' is whispering, or it's attempting to do so, practicing, flirting with chances it might be doing so, it's probably doing a little bluffing. I don't know if certain kinds of poems (I mean this kind of poem) ever say anything other than what if I get close to something by saying this, or by saying so, what if I come near. Maybe inside the poem's asking, can I come by, can I be near you. In the past two years or so I've written around sixty or so of these sonnet-length poems. It's really awe inspiring and can stop you in your tracks (and maybe leave you speechless) to see the end of a poem coming, visible and invisible, no words there yet, but a clear sense that there are no more than three or four lines to go, and you better get ready for that. The pressure is a bracing, galvanizing, thrilling problem, and before you know it, that's that. It's done. And then it's time to go looking for the next poem."

Born in New York City in November 1945, TERENCE WINCH is a poet and a musician who cofounded the traditional Irish music group Celtic Thunder in 1977. His primary instrument is the button accordion. His most recent book of poems is *Boy Drinkers* (2007). In 2011, Hanging Loose Press will publish a new collection, *Falling Out of Bed in a Room with No Floor.* Winch has released a CD of his compositions called *When New York Was Irish: Songs & Tunes by Terence Winch.* In 2009–10 he served as poet-in-residence for the high schools of Howard County, Maryland.

Of "Objects of Spiritual Significance," Winch writes: "I worked in an office for many years, and I think of this as a work poem. Throwing many diverse and often incompatible people together under one roof and expecting them to be happy and productive can sometimes seem like a crazy idea, doomed to failure by human nature. Plus, there are so many mini-apocalypses in life, all adumbrations of the big one down the road."

CATHERINE WING was born in New York City in 1972. Her first book of poems, *Enter Invisible,* was published by Sarabande Books and was nominated for a 2005 *Los Angeles Times* Book Prize. She lives in Pennsylvania and teaches at Shippensburg University.

Of "The Darker Sooner," Wing writes: "I suppose there are a number of syntactical spurs for this poem—Lewis Carroll's 'Curiouser and curiouser,' Bounty's 'the quicker picker upper'—but the final push came after I misread a line in one of my student's poems (it was something like 'In the fall it gets darker sooner'). It stuck in my head as a noun, *the* darker sooner, and the poem spun down from there."

MARK WUNDERLICH was born in Winona, Minnesota, in 1968 and grew up in rural Wisconsin near the town of Fountain City. He attended the University of Wisconsin, where he studied English and German literature, and went on to receive an MFA from Columbia University. He is the author of two collections of poems. The first, *The Anchorage,* received the Lambda Literary Award and was published by the University of Massachusetts Press in 1999. His second book, *Voluntary Servitude,* was published by Graywolf Press in 2004. He has taught at Stanford, Sarah Lawrence College, San Francisco State, and Ohio University, and now teaches at Bennington College in Vermont.

Of "Coyote, with Mange," Wunderlich writes: "I live in the Hudson Valley, on the remnants of a Colonial-era farm that abuts a larger expanse of woods and open fields of what were once dairy farms and are now fallow pastures overgrown with brush. This is home to all variety of wildlife—foxes, deer, turkeys, fishers, many birds, and a large pack of coyotes. One morning while working in the yard, I looked up the hill toward our compost heap, and looking back at me was a creature I couldn't identify. Its face seemed almost human, though malformed, disturbing. I stopped working and just stared at it while it stopped chewing and regarded me, before setting off over the hill and out of view. This poor beast had lost most of his fur, probably due to mange—a skin disease caused by mites that usually affects canines—and had been rendered into something otherworldly, strange and troubling, as it was obviously suffering.

"I grew up on a farm, and my childhood was spent tending animals, riding, hunting, and trapping. In many of my poems I have sought to illuminate the complexity of our relationship with wild and domestic creatures—something I believe is at the core of human experience—and to do this without sentimentality and with reverence and care."

MATTHEW YEAGER was born in Cincinnati, Ohio, in 1979. His first short film, *A Big Ball of Foil in a Small NY Apartment*, which he wrote and produced, screened to acclaim at various spots on the festival circuit in 2009. That same year he won the Barthelme Prize in short prose. He works for a catering company, is the cofounder of Chicken Truck Productions, and lives in Brooklyn, New York.

Of "A Jar of Balloons," Yeager writes: "This poem meanders on for twenty-five additional pages. If you'd like to read it in full, or just scroll through it, it is published online at sixthfinch/yeager2. I'm thankful to Rob McDonald at *Sixth Finch* for providing a platform for it. If you write long poems, you find yourself barred from publication—not in a mean-spirited way, but in the way a gigantic person is barred from most clothes. The Internet would seem to offer an easy solution (an instant tailoring of space), but formatting the files can be extremely tricky. I believe Rob had to use a sequence of images in iPhoto.

"As for the poem's construction, after the first ten pages, the accretion was gradual. I'd walk around, questions would occur to me, and I'd remember them or forget them. At the end of the day, or week, I'd get home and sit down and add them on. Other times I'd make them into a whole separate strand and then open the poem up, like a model train track, and fit the new section in. At different points, I was aware of the similarities between myself and the man in my poem 'A Big Ball of Foil in a Small NY Apartment,' which appeared in *The Best American Poetry 2005*. I was looking for a particular type of piece to integrate into a whole made up entirely of those pieces.

"Something like a foil scrap is limited by its physicality. If put onto a table and whispered over, it will never transform magically into ten equal-sized foil scraps. Likewise, you can't throw a found quarter at a wall and watch it firework into a $1.50 in quarters. A question, however, can turn into a series of questions. One would engender another. They would cancer outward, pollywogs of islands of questions. For whatever reason, I attempted to block this. A lot of time I had to fudge the order so the poem would maintain a patchwork quality that I liked; I didn't want there to be twenty straight questions about behavior in other people's bathrooms. I liked the poem best when it was jumping from highly specific context to highly specific context.

"How to stop? When to stop? I tend to suffer from this problem when I write poems without forms. I had about 800 questions when I felt the faucet starting to trickle; I thought a nice round shapely number, such as 1,000, might offer a logical end. I thought of 755, Hank

Aaron's home-run total, which, if you are a baseball fan, is like the Chrysler Building—not the loftiest peak in the skyline, but the best."

DEAN YOUNG was born in Columbia, Pennsylvania, in 1955. He holds the William Livingston Chair of Poetry at the University of Texas, Austin, and God help him. A book of outbursts and rambling poetics, *The Art of Recklessness,* has just been published by Graywolf Press and a new book of poems, *Fall Higher,* will be out in early 2011.

Young writes: "'Off the Hook Ode' is an attempt at trying to conjure up forgiveness, from self and everyone and all things else. I have yet to have any proof of its effectiveness, but any idiot can believe in something once it's been proved. It takes a special idiot to believe without a single clue."

KEVIN YOUNG was born in Lincoln, Nebraska, in 1970 but left before he was one year old and hasn't made it back. He did root for the Cornhuskers for much of his childhood. His first book, *Most Way Home* (William Morrow, 1995), won a National Poetry Series competition and the Zacharis First Book Award from *Ploughshares;* his third book, *Jelly Roll: A Blues* (Knopf, 2003), won the Paterson Poetry Prize; his most recent book is *Dear Darkness* (Knopf, 2008). Young has edited *The Art of Losing: Poems of Grief and Recovery,* an anthology of contemporary elegies (Bloomsbury USA, 2009). He is the Atticus Haygood Professor of Creative Writing and English and curator of Literary Collections and the Raymond Danowski Poetry Library at Emory University.

Young writes: "The poem 'Lime Light Blues' seeks what all good blues seek: laughing to keep from crying. And maybe even to get you to dance a little. Or at least sway some."

MAGAZINES WHERE THE POEMS
WERE FIRST PUBLISHED

32 Poems, eds. Deborah Ager and John Poch. PO Box 5824, Hyattsville, MD 20782.

ABZ, ed. John McKernan. PO Box 2746, Huntington, WV 25727-2746.

Action Yes Online Quarterly, eds. Johannes Göransson, Joyelle McSweeney, and John Dermot Woods. http://actionyes.org.

American Poetry Review, eds. Stephen Berg, David Bonanno, and Elizabeth Scanlon. 1700 Sansom Street, Suite 800, Philadelphia, PA 19103.

The Agriculture Reader, eds. Jeremy Schmall and Justin Taylor. c/o X-ing Books, 20 Grand Avenue, #303, Brooklyn, NY 11205.

The Antioch Review, poetry ed. Judith Hall. PO Box 148, Yellow Springs, OH 45387.

The Atlantic, poetry ed. David Barber. 600 New Hampshire Avenue, NW, Washington, DC 20008.

Boston Review, poetry eds. Timothy Donnelly and Benjamin Paloff. 35 Medford Street, Suite 302, Somerville, MA 02143.

Boulevard, ed. Richard Burgin. 6614 Clayton Road, Box 325, Richmond Heights, MO 63117.

The Brooklyn Rail, poetry ed. Anselm Berrigan. 99 Commercial Street, Suite 32, Brooklyn, NY 11222.

Callaloo, ed. Charles H. Rowell. Department of English, Texas A&M University, 4212 TAMU, College Station, TX 77843–4212.

Chicago Review, poetry ed. Michael Hansen. 5801 South Kenwood Avenue, Chicago, IL 60637.

Columbia Poetry Review, English Department, Columbia College Chicago, 600 South Michigan Avenue, Chicago, IL 60605.

Conduit, ed. William Waltz. 510 Eighth Avenue NE, Minneapolis, MN 55413.

Court Green, eds. Tony Trigilio and David Trinidad. Columbia College Chicago, 600 South Michigan Avenue, Chicago, IL 60605.

Double Room, ed. Mark Tursi. http://doubleroomjournal.com.

FIELD, eds. David Young and David Walker. Oberlin College Press, 50 North Professor Street, Oberlin, OH 44074.

Five Points, eds. David Bottoms and Megan Sexton. PO Box 3999, Atlanta, GA 30302–3999.

The Georgia Review, ed. Stephen Corey. The University of Georgia, Athens, GA 30602–9009.

Harper's, literary ed. Ben Metcalf. http://harpers.org.

The Hat, eds. Jordan Davis and Chris Edgar. Submissions@hatpoetry .com.

The Hudson Review, ed. Paula Dietz. 684 Park Avenue, New York, NY 10021.

Image, ed. Gregory Wolfe. 3307 Third Avenue West, Seattle, WA 98119.

LIT, poetry ed. Graeme Bezanson. The New School, Writing Program, Room 514, 66 West 12th Street, New York, NY 10011.

London Review of Books, ed. Mary-Kay Wilmers. 28 Little Russell Street, London WC1A 2HN.

Michigan Quarterly Review, ed. Jonathan Freedman. 0576 Rackham Bldg., 915 East Washington Street, Ann Arbor, MI 48109–1070.

MiPOesias, ed. Didi Menendez. www.mipoesias.com.

New England Review, poetry ed. C. Dale Young. Middlebury College, Middlebury, VT 05753.

The New Yorker, poetry ed. Paul Muldoon. 4 Times Square, New York, NY 10036.

The New York Quarterly, ed. Raymond Hammond. PO Box 2015, Old Chelsea Station, New York, NY 10113.

Open City, eds. Thomas Beller and Joanna Yas. 270 Lafayette Street, Suite 1412, New York, NY 10012.

The Oxford American, ed. Marc Smirnoff. 201 Donaghey Avenue, Main 107, Conway, AR 72035. www.oxfordamerican.org.

Pleiades, eds. Kevin Prufer and Wayne Miller. Department of English, University of Central Missouri, Warrensburg, MO 64093.

Ploughshares, poetry ed. John Skoyles. Emerson College, 120 Boylston Street, Boston, MA 02116–4624.

Poetry, ed. Christian Wiman. 444 North Michigan Avenue, Suite 1850, Chicago, IL 60611–4034.

Poets & Writers, ed. Kevin Larimer. www.pw.org/magazine.

Prairie Schooner, ed.-in-chief Hilda Raz. 201 Andrews Hall, PO Box 880334, Lincoln, NE 68588–0334.

A Public Space, poetry eds. Dan Beachy-Quick, Edwin Frank, and Brett Fletcher Lauer. 323 Dean Street, Brooklyn, NY 11217.

Sentence, ed. Brian Clements. Box 7, Western Connecticut State University, 181 White Street, Danbury, CT 06810.

Sewanee Review, ed. George Core. University of the South, 735 University Avenue, Sewanee, TN 37383–1000.

Sewanee Theological Review, ed. Kevin Williamson. School of Theology, Box 46-W, Sewanee, TN 37383–0001.

The Sienese Shredder, eds. Brice Brown and Trevor Winkfield. 344 West 23rd Street, #4D, New York, NY 10011. http://sienese-shredder.com.

Sixth Finch, ed. Rob MacDonald. www.sixthfinch.com.

Sonora Review, Department of English, University of Arizona, Tucson, AZ 85721.

Southern Poetry Review, ed. Robert Parham. Department of Languages, Literature and Philosophy, Armstrong Atlantic State University, 11935 Abercorn Street, Savannah, GA 31419–1997.

Tin House, poetry ed. Brenda Shaughnessy. PO Box 10500, Portland, OR 97210.

Vanitas, ed. Vincent Katz. 211 West 19th Street, #5, New York, NY 10011.

Verse, eds. Brian Henry and Andrew Zawacki. English Department, University of Richmond, Richmond, VA 23173.

The Virginia Quarterly Review, ed. Ted Genoways. One West Range, Box 400223, Charlottesville, VA 22904–4223.

West Branch, ed. Paula Closson Buck. Bucknell University, 701 Moore Avenue, Lewisburg, PA 17837.

Witness, poetry ed. Joshua Kryah. Black Mountain Institute, University of Nevada, Las Vegas, NV 89154–5085.

Women's Review of Books, ed. Amy Hoffman. Wellesley Centers for Women, Wellesley College, 106 Central Street, Wellesley, MA 02481.

ACKNOWLEDGMENTS

The series editor wishes to thank Mark Bibbins for his invaluable assistance. I am grateful as well to Mary Jo Bang, Jill Baron, Jaclyn Clark, Julia Cohen, Denise Duhamel, Elaine Equi, Allison Green, Stacey Harwood, Jennifer Michael Hecht, Richard Howard, Elizabeth Howort, Jamie Katz, Ben Mirov, Kathleen Ossip, Angela Patrinos, Michael Schiavo, and Paul Violi. Warm thanks go, as always, to Glen Hartley and Lynn Chu of Writers' Representatives; to copyeditor David Stanford Burr; and to Alexis Gargagliano, my editor, Erich Hobbing, Kelsey Smith, and Daniel Cuddy of Scribner.

Grateful acknowledgment is made to the magazines in which these poems first appeared and the magazine editors who selected them. A sincere attempt has been made to locate all copyright holders. Unless otherwise noted, copyright to the poems is held by the individual poets.

Dick Allen: "What You Have to Get Over" appeared in *The Hudson Review*. Reprinted by permission of the poet.

John Ashbery: "Alcove" from *Planisphere*. © 2009 by John Ashbery. Reprinted by permission of Ecco/HarperCollins. Also appeared in *London Review of Books*.

Sandra Beasley: "Unit of Measure" from *I Was the Jukebox*. © 2010 by Sandra Beasley. Reprinted by permission of W. W. Norton and Co. Also appeared in *Poetry*.

Mark Bibbins: "The Devil You Don't" from *The Dance of No Hard Feelings*. © 2009 by Mark Bibbins. Reprinted by permission of Copper Canyon Press. Also appeared in *The New York Quarterly*.

Todd Boss: "My Dog Has No Nose" appeared in *The Georgia Review*. Reprinted by permission of the poet.

Fleda Brown: "The Dead" appeared in *Southern Poetry Review*. Reprinted by permission of the poet.

Anne Carson: "Wildly Constant" appeared in *London Review of Books*. Reprinted by permission of the poet.

Tom Clark: "Fidelity" from *The New World*. © 2009 by Tom Clark. Reprinted by permission of Libellum. Also appeared in *Vanitas*.

David Clewell: "This Poem Had Better Be about the World We Actu-